Renewing Civic Capacity:

Preparing College Students for Service and Citizenship

by Suzanne W. Morse

ASHE-ERIC Higher Education Report 8, 1989

Prepared by

Clearinghouse on Higher Education
The George Washington University

In cooperation with

ASHE

Association for the Study
of Higher Education

Published by

School of Education and Human Development
The George Washington University

Jonathan D. Fife, Series Editor

Cite as

Morse, Suzanne W. *Renewing Civic Capacity: Preparing College Students for Service and Citizenship.* ASHE-ERIC Higher Education Report No. 8. Washington, D.C.: School of Education and Human Development, The George Washington University, 1989.

Library of Congress Catalog Card Number 89-063528
ISSN 0884-0040
ISBN 0-9623882-7-0

Managing Editor: Christopher Rigaux
Manuscript Editor: Barbara Fishel/Editech
Cover design by Michael David Brown, Rockville, Maryland

The ERIC Clearinghouse on Higher Education invites individuals to submit proposals for writing monographs for the *ASHE-ERIC Higher Education Report* series. Proposals must include:
1. A detailed manuscript proposal of not more than five pages.
2. A chapter-by-chapter outline.
3. A 75-word summary to be used by several review committees for the initial screening and rating of each proposal.
4. A vita and a writing sample.

ERIC Clearinghouse on Higher Education
School of Education and Human Development
The George Washington University
One Dupont Circle, Suite 630
Washington, DC 20036-1183

This publication was prepared partially with funding from the Office of Educational Research and Improvement, U.S. Department of Education, under contract no. ED RI-88-062014. The opinions expressed in this report do not necessarily reflect the positions or policies of OERI or the Department.

EXECUTIVE SUMMARY

America faces mounting problems. As the nation approaches
the 21st century, citizens must tackle an enormous national
debt, respond to the many people who live in poverty, and
lessen the environmental damage that threatens the future
of our air and our atmosphere. We may, however, be faced
with an even bigger problem: the loss of civic participation
to meet these challenges. Despite the technological expertise
that narrows geographical barriers, citizens have become more
and more alienated from each other at a time when we need
each other most. Jean-Jacques Rousseau said, "We have physicists, geometers, chemists, astronomers, poets, musicians,
painters; we no longer have citizens . . ." (1964, p. 19). Rousseau's dire observation defines the civic crisis today, which
wills to the next generation of citizens a society with stran-
gling problems and only limited skills to address them. The
history of higher education in America has a rich tradition
of preparing students for their civic roles and responsibilities.
With increased specialization, however, the words in many
mission statements—"to prepare competent and responsible
citizens for democratic society"—have lost their emphasis
in the curriculum.

What Is Citizenship and Public Life?

Citizenship is more than a legal construct with clearly defined
individual rights and responsibilities. The concept goes
beyond what we do and think as individuals to a common
way of thinking about our shared interests and common life.
When Alexis de Tocqueville visited America in 1831, he
observed that:

> *These Americans are the most peculiar people in the world.
> You'll not believe it when I tell you how they behave. In a
> local community in their country, a citizen may conceive
> of some need [that] is not being met. What does he do?
> He goes across the street and discusses it with his neighbor.
> Then what happens? A committee begins functioning on
> behalf of that need. All of this is done by private citizens
> on their own initiative. The health of a democratic society
> may be measured by the quality of functions performed
> by private citizens* (1956, p. 201).

It is this spirit of citizens conferring with citizens that is missing today.

This brand of direct democracy was built on the notion of the Greek *polis,* where the citizen's first priority was to participate in public life. While Americans never participated so directly, the New England town meeting, which Thomas Jefferson called "the wisest invention ever devised by man" (1903, vol. 8, p. 203), did allow for direct participation. While these early models excluded many individuals and lacked the balance between individual rights, they are helpful metaphorically, because citizenship today, despite the context of a highly technological, bureaucratic world, requires that individuals be knowledgeable of the public problems but, more important, have the capacity to act together toward their solutions. Modern citizenship requires participation in the public life almost by default. Our lives, no matter how individualistic, are affected by public decisions every day. The concept that individuals who are productive in society have an integrated private and public life is the foundation for building a new cadre of citizens.

> *We misunderstand public life if we equate it with politics, with the activities of government. Not only do we misunderstand it, we also strangle our sense of public possibilities. The heart of public life is simply the interaction of strangers and that is a basic and vital human experience, not a specialized political process* (Palmer 1981, p. 22).

The kind of public life we have depends on the kind of people we are. Tocqueville's account of his visit to America examined the American character today, which he called at times "habits of the heart." A retracing of that visit found that citizens today are people who have much in common and believe, despite many obstacles, that community and commitment could be renewed in America (Bellah et al. 1985).

What Is Higher Education's Role in Educating for Citizenship?

A democratic citizenry, required by Thomas Jefferson, should be well educated and informed on the issues of the day, with the necessary skills to participate. Citizens must feel that they hold office in the country and have mastered a set of skills and competencies. Early American colleges considered "responsible citizenship" part of their mission as they developed learned gentlemen capable of providing informed leadership for the new country. With industrialization and urbanization of America in the late 19th and early 20th centuries, however, emphasis shifted to preparing individuals with the specialized skills and knowledge to contribute to and guide the burgeoning America. Despite the waning interest, colleges and universities have a mandate to develop responsible citizens.

> *At its best, the campus is expected to bring together the views and experiences of all its points of view and create something greater than the sum, offering the prospect that personal values will be clarified and the channels of our common life will be deepened and renewed* (Boyer and Hechinger 1981, p. 56).

We must, however, find ways to balance individual needs and larger public purposes (Boyer 1988). Said another way, the challenge for education is to develop citizens. The issue is, how? A number of ways have very strong arguments and advocates. Six general categories can be used to frame the debate: (1) cultural traditions and classical education; (2) community and public service and experiential education; (3) studies of leadership; (4) general and liberal arts education; (5) civic or public leadership education; and (6) "other," which includes professional education, international studies, and philanthropy. These approaches to civic education are based on certain premises of the public life and democratic theory. Individuals learn about citizenship and its role in the public realm throughout their lives. Relearning new notions about citizenship will require new ways of thinking, relating, and acting. Higher education can help students develop civic skills and create the experience of civic life during very critical formative years.

This development can be encouraged in a variety of ways and in a number of places. Faculty, administrators, students, and the broader community can work together in defining what it means to be a civic community. What higher education offers to the process is a setting, a curriculum, and an established community, all aimed at developing human beings for living in a public world. It is important that the higher education community, in toto, think together about how to define, address, and develop the next generation of citizen leaders. Jefferson reminded us of the importance:

I know of no safe depository of the ultimate powers of the society but the people themselves; and if we think them not enlightened enough to exercise control with a wholesome discretion, the remedy is not to take it from them, but to inform their discretion by education (1903, vol. 8, p. 278).

What Are the Skills for a Renewed Civic Life?

"Our political behavior depends on our idea of what democracy is, can be, and should be" (Sartori 1987, p. 12). We learn our notions of it from our relationships and interactions with parents, teachers, peers, the media, and our history, and these impressions mold visions of democracy and determine how we see the citizen's role in relationship to it. Three models can be used to define that role: *electoral-competitive, representative,* and *participatory democracy.* Each requires different attitudes, skills, and levels of participation and interaction.

The more expansive model, participatory democracy, requires first and foremost active participation. It also requires the civic skills of public talk, public judgment, thinking, imagination, and the courage to act. Briefly, public talk requires that citizens have the ability to talk, listen, *and* act together for common purposes. What citizens learn from talking with each other are *new* ways of relating and working with others. Public talk is prerequisite for public judgment, which requires both thinking and imagining. "Judgment is the ability to bring principles to particulars without reducing the particulars to simple instances" (Minnich 1988, p. 33). Political judgment requires the ability to think together with others about what the right public course of action should be. It is not a solo activity; it requires that others be recognized and acknowledged in the process. "The journey from private opinion to political judgment does not follow a road from prejudices to true knowledge; it proceeds from solitude to sociability" (Barber 1988, p. 199). Public judgment is the capacity to think with others about collective lives and actions. It requires the ability to talk or imagine different viewpoints and perspectives with others.

College and university communities are in the special position of deciding what responsible citizenship requires in a democratic society and the skills that are required for it. To begin this process, conversations on campus must address these issues and how the curriculum can best inculcate them. Colleges and universities can help students to refine and expand their notions of citizenship and the common world through the classroom and how it is structured, by providing opportunities for experiential learning, and in creating a campus community where all constituencies can think together about their shared lives. The challenge, however, is not about what kind of curriculum, governance, or extracurricular activities are in place. It is about finding ways to solve the problems that face the world we share.

ADVISORY BOARD

Roger G. Baldwin
Assistant Professor of Education
College of William and Mary

Carol M. Boyer
Consultant and Senior Academic Planner
Massachusetts Board of Regents of Higher Education

Ellen Earle Chaffee
Associate Commissioner of Academic Affairs
North Dakota State Board of Higher Education

Martin Finkelstein
Associate Professor of Higher Education Administration
Seton Hall University

Carol Everly Floyd
Associate Vice Chancellor for Academic Affairs
Board of Regents of the Regency Universities System
State of Illinois

George D. Kuh
Professor of Higher Education
Indiana University

Yvonna S. Lincoln
Associate Professor of Higher Education
University of Kansas

Michael A. Olivas
Professor of Law
University of Houston

Richard F. Wilson
Associate Chancellor
University of Illinios

Ami Zusman
Principal Analyst, Academic Affairs
University of California

CONSULTING EDITORS

Leonard L. Baird
Professor
University of Kentucky

James H. Banning
Associate Professor of Psychology
Colorado State University

Trudy W. Banta
Research Professor
University of Tennessee

Margaret J. Barr
Vice Chancellor for Student Affairs
Texas Christian University

Louis W. Bender
Director, State and Regional Higher Education Center
Florida State University

Larry Braskamp
Associate Vice Chancellor for Academic Affairs
University of Illinois

L. Leon Campbell
Provost and Vice President for Academic Affairs
University of Delaware

Darrell Clowes
Associate Professor of Education
Viginia Tech

Susan Cohen
Associate, Project for Collaborative Learning
Lesley College

John W. Creswell
Professor and Lilly Project Director
University of Nebraska

Mary E. Dilworth
Director, Research and Information Services
ERIC Clearinghouse on Teacher Education

James A. Eison
Director, Center for Teaching and Learning
Southeast Missouri State University

Lawrence Erickson
Professor and Coordinator of Reading and Language Studies
Southern Illinois University

Valerie French
Professor of History
American University

J. Wade Gilley
Senior Vice President
George Mason University

Milton Greenberg
Provost
American University

Judith Dozier Hackman
Associate Dean
Yale University

Brian L. Hawkins
Vice President for Computing and Information Sciences
Brown University

Joseph V. Julian
Public Affairs and Alumni Relations
Syracuse University

Oscar T. Lenning
Vice President for Academic Affairs
Robert Wesleyan College

Jeanne M. Likens
Director, Commuter Student Affairs
Ohio State University

James W. Lyons
Dean of Student Affairs
Stanford University

Judith B. McLaughlin
Research Associate on Education and Sociology
Harvard University

Sherry Magill
Vice President and Deputy to the President
Washington College

CONTENTS

FOREWORD

Congress is often considered a delayed mirror of our society's needs and wants. Because the Congressional members are concerned about being re-elected, they rarely present bills they feel will not receive approval by a majority of their constituency. Thus, the high number of bills (18) promoting public service which were presented during the 1989 Congress indicate a growing national call for the establishment of incentives for individual participation in civic activities.

There are many indicators of decreased involvement in civic activities. For example, the drop in the percentage of eligible population voting in local "off-year" elections, membership in service organizations, and per-capita involvement with the sick and homeless. This trend is also evidenced in the annual survey of freshmen. *The American Freshman: National Norms for Fall, 1989* found that 59.7 percent of the students identified the helping of others in need as an objective they considered to be "essential" or "very important." However, only 26.1 percent thought involvement in environmental clean-up action was "essential" or "very important," and 23.3 percent felt the same about participation in community action.

A number of theories seek to explain this situation. One holds that many of our community functions have become less personal, causing a feeling that individuals cannot make a difference. Another cites a lowering of personal and national self-esteem, and another blames the unwillingness of schools and parents to make civic participation a valued activity. This last theory can be clearly seen at the higher education level where many faculty pride themselves in being "value free"; where ethics and community service are considered minor, if not nonexistent, elements of the curriculum; and where the third mission of higher education—service—is narrowly defined and is generally not part of the reward structure.

Suzanne W. Morse, Director of Programs at the Charles F. Kettering Foundation, carefully reviews the issue of citizenship and civic education in this report. Dr. Morse presents a helpful analysis of the skills of citizenship and models of political life. She concludes her presentation with specific implications for faculty, administrators and students.

Many factors determine the cultural norms and values of a higher education institution and its curriculum. Often a particular value that contributes to the culture goes unexamined. The time is right to review the value of preparing college students for citizenship and service. This report will provide a useful foundation for such an analysis.

Jonathan D. Fife
Series Editor and Professor of Higher Education
Director, ERIC Clearinghouse on Higher Education
School of Education and Human Development
The George Washington University

ACKNOWLEDGMENTS

Two people deserve tremendous credit for this report: Patricia Ginan, who tirelessly typed and proofed the manuscript while encouraging the author, and Katina Manko, who assisted with the primary research and editing in a scholarly, exhaustive way. Both were critical to this project, and both have retained their good humor.

Several people shared their thoughts with me in conversations on this topic: Norman Cousins, David Mathews, Elizabeth Minnich, and Bernard Murchland, in particular. A special acknowledgment is due NEXT GENERATION, the group that showed me a new way to think about community and this world we share.

INTRODUCTION

America is soon to enter a new millennium and a new era in its history. Along with unprecedented technological developments, the country is faced with huge public problems. Americans cannot or will not pay the national debt. The country has millions of poor, hungry, homeless fellow citizens, and environmental conditions threaten the health of future generations. These complex issues are not just national problems: They are local and international ones as well. Their complexities reveal more than ever the inability of government—any government—to find solutions. Actions will have to be broader based and inclusive. Social problems will require that individual citizens work together and within communities and organizations to develop the capacity for addressing the critical public issues that face the country. The advent of a more complex society coupled with the increasing alienation of people, particularly younger Americans, calls for new approaches for reconnecting citizens with the larger public world.

Few Americans see participating in civic affairs as part of their responsibilities.

Evidence of this alienation is obvious from the statistics. Very few Americans see participating in civic affairs as part of their responsibilities as citizens (Pitkin 1981, p. 327). A study of college freshmen indicates that only 25 percent of college freshmen believe that participating in community action is very important, compared to almost 80 percent who believe that it is "very important" to be well off financially (Astin et al. 1988). Voting for some has become the ultimate measure of participation, but less than 20 percent of eligible voters aged 18 to 24 voted in the 1986 congressional election, compared to 37 percent of total registered voters. Simply increasing the voting statistics is not likely to enfranchise younger people or any other group to think and act together on the future of the country. The critical task before the nation is to invigorate the notion of dialogue between citizens and problem solving at every level of American public life.

This transformation in American civic life will require the efforts of every American institution, from the family to the church. It may be the educational community, with its heritage and access, however, that provides the greatest hope for preparing the next generation of citizens. John Dewey reminded us that "democracy has to be born anew every generation, and education is the midwife" (Curti 1965, p. 499). Colleges and universities have the opportunity to help younger citizens in their early adult years develop the skills and understanding of citizenship that will influence their civic lives. The need for education in citizenship has been a dominant theme in American public life since the country's beginnings. Led by Jefferson, the founders emphasized this need: "I know of no safe depository of the ultimate powers of the society but the people themselves; and if we think them not enlightened enough to exercise control with a wholesome discretion, the remedy is not to take it from them, but to inform their discretion by education" (1903, p. 278).

This Jeffersonian notion of a democracy sustained by a nation of informed citizens seemed more possible in a time when values and views were more widely shared. The communal part of American life that Alexis de Tocqueville admired in the 1830s seems remote from society today. Despite the great changes in the way democratic ideas are practiced and expressed, education must still play a primary role in the preparation of citizens (Boyer and Hechinger 1981, p. 43).

Colleges and universities are only one set of organizations that can affect the development and encourage the practice of civic skills. They cannot solve all of society's ills. But what they can do above all else is to provide the theory, the practice, and the place for civic learning. The college years may be the last time that students have both the luxury and the opportunity to think critically about the values and skills needed for an active civic life. Educational institutions, through formal education or cocurricular activities, have the access, opportunity, structure, and environment to prepare students for responsible citizenship by helping define and develop the skills, tools, and perceptions of our common, democratic life. The academy can create a community and a way of learning that allows students to experience a different kind of civic or political life. The civic function of higher education can be persuasively argued:

> . . . not that the university has a civic mission but that the university is a civic mission, is a civility itself, defined as the rules and conventions that permit a community to facilitate conversation and the kinds of discourse upon which all knowledge depends (Barber 1989, pp. 67–68).

One of the missing pieces within civic learning is therefore an environment in which individuals can experience and practice citizenship. The kinds of special interest and governmental regulatory politics that the media report day after day have caused many citizens to separate themselves from any kind of interaction with others that is not either of personal interest or confrontational. The NIMBY rule of politics (not in *my* backyard) governs all levels of interaction. Philosopher Hannah Arendt said that personal interaction, dialogue, and debate are the essence of politics but that citizens must have a space to develop the skills to participate. And the necessary public space "comes into being *in between* human beings," allowing them to meet as equals on issues of common concern (Arendt, cited in Bernstein 1986, p. 36). The opportunity for higher education is that it can be that public space for all of its constituencies, but particularly for students. The campus, the classroom, and the community can be spaces for students and faculty to think together about local, national, and international concerns. The collegial environment offers students a place to question, to participate, to develop civic skills, and to respect and understand the pluralistic world in which they live. The increased emphasis on community service provides many opportunities for practicing politics. The challenge for educators is to find ways in today's world to reinvigorate the discussion and redefinition of the classical notion of politics, where private citizens saw as their responsibility, in tandem with others, the discussion and resolution of public problems. Pericles gave this charge best in 430 B.C.:

> *Our Constitution favors the many instead of the few; this is why it is called a democracy .... Our people have, besides politics, their private affairs to attend to, and our ordinary citizens, though occupied with the pursuits of industry, are still fair judges of public matters; for, unlike any other nation, [we regard] him who takes no part in these duties not as unambitious but as useless, and instead of evoking discussion as a stumbling block in the way of action, we think it an indispensable preliminary to any action at all* (1811, pp. 37–40).

It has been said more recently that citizens' participation is a duty; moreover, the enjoyment of democratic rights depends on that duty. Theodore Roosevelt's notion of "fellow-feeling"—mutual respect and kindness in the public realm—comes when people have common objectives (1956, p. 279). Our civic selves are defined not by municipalities or governments but by these relations with other people. The *polis* is, properly speaking, not the city/state in its physical location but the organization of the people as it rises out of acting and speaking together, and its true space lies between people living together for this purpose (Arendt 1958, pp. 51–52).

Creating this "fellow feeling"—an informed citizenry that is willing to think and act together—is the public challenge of the future. Inherent in this challenge are the economic and social realities of a country that can be defined by sectionalism, ethnicity, and economics rather than by any common goals. The driving issue is how such a society of citizen leaders can be created. Obviously, many answers are possible. Certain identifiable skills and perceptions about a citizen's role and responsibility must first be defined and encouraged, however.

The purposes of this monograph are to define responsible citizenship in a democratic society and its requisite skills, to review higher education's role in civic education, to identify ways colleges and universities can help develop the skills and requirements of citizenship and public life, and to present ways that campuses through teaching, governance, extracurricular activities, campus life, and community relations can create a new environment for learning about the civic life.

The nation began with a rich heritage on which to associate and build a new *and* renewed civic society; our founders expanded our understanding of what a citizen can and should be. While writers from Pericles on have built their description of civic life on a society segregated by race and gender and means, however, today's society cannot tolerate or operate on a system of citizenship that is exclusive. Rather, we have learned the importance of many voices through increased political access for minorities and women over the last 25 years. Collectively, this nation and the world hold the ideas, initiative, and ability to move society forward.

For more than 300 years, higher education has been a vehicle by which the next generation of citizen leaders learn about their public responsibilities. It is important—essential—that the role and responsibility of civic life be redefined and renewed.

THE CITIZEN'S ROLE IN AMERICAN PUBLIC LIFE

Citizenship has become almost a hollow phrase to most Americans, receiving the most attention when a perceived right or privilege is threatened. This situation was especially true a few years ago, when reports showed large numbers of foreign workers and families migrating into America's urban and rural areas, capturing a large number of jobs and crowding the school and welfare systems. The call for the protection of citizenship was loud and clear. While the U.S. Constitution and the Bill of Rights do not define citizenship, citizenship is a legal construct that implies membership, rights, responsibilities, and protections, a mutual relationship between citizens and state. We are all born into the profession of citizenship, like it or not, exercise it or not (Gagnon 1988). On its face, this statement is correct. But being part of the civic fabric of society carries with it more than birth. Using the argument that our private lives and public lives are interconnected, Aristotle said that individuals are not "citizens" separate from their everyday lives (Barker 1946). Citizenship is neither a grand scheme for securing public office nor something that can be fulfilled just by exercising the vote or by obeying all the laws. It is all of them, yet none of them.

Citizenship is not an abstract concept—quite the contrary. Individuals think about the role of citizen in very tangible ways—"I am a citizen after all!"—to indicate that the position they hold is real and recognizable. Although the commonly held definition refers to the "rights" of citizenship, its original conception was much more than that, and the term "citizenship" has specific connotations. It is derived from the words city and *civitas*. Some writers argue that it means the "right to act in the public realm" (Kelly 1979, p. 27), while others take that notion a step farther, noting that the most important fact about citizens is that they are defined as members of a political community (Barber 1984). The civic identity is intended only when citizens interact with other citizens in mutual ways (p. 200). Therefore, citizenship is not just about the rights of an individual; it also involves the interactions and responsibilities of all citizens in a democratic society. For citizenship to be renewed, an awakening of the *office of citizen* must occur (Ketcham 1987, p. 145).

With this civic renewal comes the necessity to think about how individuals learn to be citizens. The old forms of patriotic metaphors, such as Uncle Sam and waving the flag, are not enough to meet the needs of a highly technical, industrialized world. The goal must be a renewed *civic consciousness,* a process that involves personal commitment to public interests and is aimed toward molding obligations and attachments into a higher order of citizenship (Janowitz 1983, pp. x–xi).

The role of citizen is defined in part by the vision held of the democratic system. The belief that sovereign authority in any democracy rests with the people, for example, emphasizes the importance of that role. In a democratic system, the *citizen* is the ruler and the arbiter. To fulfill these responsibilities, citizens should "have a measure of careful education, the high sense of duty and obligation, the disinterestedness to allow for judgment, and the deliberate training and apprenticeship always assumed essential for a good ruler, at least if the society is to experience wise and virtuous government" (Ketcham 1987, p. 145). Given this vision, citizenship is an ongoing participative process, not a static one. It requires the ability to reflect, understand, and decide together. Without these skills and direct involvement, citizens cannot effectively deal with change or make the informed choices needed for a healthy democratic life.

The worst scenario is that citizens would become so frustrated trying to deal with complex changes that they would ultimately withdraw from their civic responsibilities and refuse to participate at all (Lazerson, McLaughlin, and McPherson 1984). When citizenship takes a back seat to private gains and special interests, the collective good is lost among the indictments of "meism" and private interests. As early as the 18th century, the philosopher Jean-Jacques Rousseau warned, "We have physicists, geometers, chemists, astronomers, poets, musicians, painters; we no longer have citizens" (1964, p. 19).

In some ways, that description applies exactly to modern citizenship. The problems that face the nation—debt, environment, social services—are so complex that most people cannot digest the basic facts, let alone propose possible solutions. Problems are mangled with jargon, bureaucratic tie-ups, and political rhetoric that cause many citizens to throw up their hands in disgust or pursue more individual, special interests. The state has simply outgrown the human reach and understanding of its citizens. It is not necessarily monstrous, divided, or subjugated, but its citizens are alienated and powerless, experiencing a kind of moral uneasiness (Walzer 1971, p. 204).

The antidote, the notion of a common life, has been left
at the starting gate. The term "common good," however, can
be the tripping point. Searching for the "common" leads people to questions about values, diversity, and power. The description of collective civic life, however, helps clarify the
point. Like it or not, believe it or not, citizens share collective
air and water, collective social service systems, and collective
national debt. It is inescapable. The task then is to have people understand what is shared and "common" between us
and then to move conversation toward respecting diverse
thoughts and opinions. Further, the civic goal is both to prepare people to act as responsible citizens and to carve out
ways that meaningful participation is feasible and possible.

The difficulty of calling people to act on public issues
results in part from a more endemic problem: special interests. The need is great to move people and ideas from the
personal context to the public context. The well-known
phrase "think globally, act locally" gets at the genesis of this
dilemma. As communities and nations have become more
interdependent, the domino effect of public policy decisions
becomes all the more apparent. What are the ingredients of
civic education that move people, communities, and nations
beyond their special interests to collective interests? One way
is that public problems, even ones being dealt with locally,
need a larger context. Public policy issues are like the highway
system. Lanes, county roads, state roads, intercity beltways,
and interstate highways make up the system; each is an extension of the other with all building to a transportation system.
The same could be said of the environment, world health,
and the myriad issues being addressed at every level. To educate people to think nationally is a mistake. Students must
understand the American context certainly, but they must
appreciate this nation's interdependence with others as well.

The dilemma in higher education is the ever-present tension of meeting students' individual needs while giving them
a larger global context (Boyer 1988). The community dimension encourages students to reach beyond their private interests, learn about the global, interdependent society, and
develop a sense of civic responsibility that will enable them
to contribute to society. It is critical that the balance between
individual and community be maintained, and the synergistic
relationship between the two is the ultimate goal (pp. 67,

296). According to Tocqueville, "Citizens who are bound to take part in public affairs must turn from their private interests and occasionally take a look at something other than themselves" (Mayer 1969, p. 510).

Origins of Citizen Participation

Part of Alexis de Tocqueville's America was neighbor talking to neighbor. That was mid-19th century, however, when towns were small and situations more manageable. The total population in the United States in 1820 was fewer than 10 million, compared with 248 million today. Direct democracy, as it is considered today, had its origins in Ancient Greece, where citizens were expected to participate in public life as their first priority. The notion of politics and the political community and the role of Greek citizens were very different from today. In fact, this direct democracy may have been possible only in the ancient city-*polis* (Jaeger 1939, p. 48). Actually, fifth century democracy was referred to as "the democracy of the club." Only about 21,000 Athenian citizens were considered citizens, scarcely 5 percent of the total population (Reichley 1985, p. 43).

The Greeks provide some lessons for describing politics in today's democracy, however. They, after all, coined the notion of the *polis* and the interrelationship of public lives with private lives for the modern world. The Greek *polis* was a place where citizens could come together as equals to discuss affairs of state. The public realm "gathers us together and prevents our falling all over each other" (Arendt 1958, p. 52). This public space allows citizens the opportunity to have a place for relating to and discussing the public interest.

This *polis* of Ancient Greece was not the implied city-state at all; rather, it was a city-community called a *koinonia*. Referring to the Greek system of government as a democratic state is conceptually and terminologically inaccurate (Sartori 1987), for the primary characteristic of the Greek state was just the reverse: It was stateless, and it held different goals and values from the way government is thought of today. This brand of democracy was direct, so much so, in fact, that citizens lived in a symbiotic relationship with the *polis*. Government, as the Greeks practiced it, required complete devotion to public service. The citizen's first responsibility was to the *polis;* his private life was secondary. As it turned out, economic atrophy evolved from this political hypertrophy. The more the Greek citizen participated, the poorer he became:

> For the Greeks, "man" and "citizen" meant exactly the same thing, just as participating in the life of the polis of their city meant "to live." This is not to say, of course, that the polites *did not enjoy individual liberty in the sense of a private space existing de facto. . . . The Greek* idion *(private), in contrast to* koinon *(the common element), conveys the sense of privation and lack even more strongly. . . . The Latin* privatus, *i.e., private, [meaning] "deprived". . . was used to connote an existence that was incomplete and defective in relation to the community. . . . In the classical formula of democracy, the community allows no margin of independence. . . . The* polis *is sovereign in the sense that the individuals that compose it are completely subject to it* (Sartori 1987, pp. 284–86).

The government of Athens was direct democracy "by the people" (Jaeger 1939, p. 111). It was not a representative version in the slightest. Inculcated in the citizenry were the executive, judicial, and legislative functions of government. The *polis* was the place where "each individual is given his due place in its political cosmos, . . . thereby [giving] him besides his private life, a sort of second life." This notion of the balance between public and private lives calls for a citizen not only to sympathize and cooperate with others in the *polis* but also to be responsible for his daily work. The new dimension in the development of the city-state was exactly this balance. It was quite different from the State Plato described in the *Republic* as one of legal order ruled by a few superior men. On the contrary, in the *polis,* each man was a political being and was expected to take an active role in the affairs of his community and to recognize and accept the civic duties demanded by his public self. The ideal state that Pericles spoke of was one where average citizens joined the aristocracy in executing the civic life of the community (Jaeger 1939, pp. 111–12).

The Greeks should not be judged too harshly. In the 2,000 years since the establishment of the *polis,* civilization has evolved and clarified its values. During this interim, the Western World has experienced a range of major ideological and religious movements, from Christianity to the Reformation to natural law, and has gained from the influences of the process (Sartori 1987, p. 279). But we did not lose a civic paradise when Athens fell (Ignatieff 1984, p. 107). While the nostalgic notions of direct governance still pervade, a clear realization exists that what the Greeks had in ancient Athens and the Italians during the Renaissance was steeped in contrary traditions, such as slavery, crime, and feuding factions. It does not dim our desire for what could have been, however.

The History of American Citizenship

When America won her independence from England, the nation had for some years encountered numerous fits and starts in defining the new nation. Thomas Jefferson, an early architect of the nation, contended that to be called "citizen," every member of the community must be involved in the business of society. He believed that citizenship meant membership in the larger community—being a member of the "public." The notion of community was a tangible, definable concept in Jefferson's day. People lived in geographical communities and participated with their neighbors in their collective affairs. Their deliberations and conclusions were part of the public interest, which was one of the reasons that Jefferson insisted that ward-republics be established in each county so that each citizen could participate in the affairs of the community (Matthews 1984, p. 83). The vehicle for participation by citizens he proposed was the model of the New England town meeting, where citizens gathered to do the business of the community. In a letter to Samuel Kercheval, he called them "the wisest invention ever devised by the wit of man." The ward-republics, designed around the town meeting, cemented the whole "by giving to every citizen, personally, a part in the administration of public affairs" (Jefferson 1903, vol. 8, p. 203). His contemporary, Edmund Burke, endorsed the "little platoons" of democracy—family, church, and community. This early form of democracy taught the virtue of public life through these face-to-face encounters (O'Neil 1987, p. 12).

Like the Greek *polis,* these notions of participatory meetings were not perfect by any means, nor did the likes of Madison, Adams, and Payne agree to them. They never wanted a direct democracy and did not want the republican form of government accepted as a substitute for one. For the most part, the founders viewed direct democracy as impractical, undesirable, and dangerous. Even Edmund Burke, who was an architect of this representative model, held that direct democracy would limit and exclude minorities from rights and participation. The framers felt that the representative form of government they proposed would guard against special interest politics that would result from localism, factions, and imprudent majoritarianism. Democracy, they believed, could work only in small communities. Representation allowed for an extended republic (Cronin 1989, pp. 22–28). The primary purpose of the early forms of direct democracy, however, was not individual representation but the homogeneity and tranquility of the community. Dissenters were banned, and this early "peculiar democracy" was actually built on group demands of consensus, compromise, and conformity. This model limited individual rights well into the 18th century (Zuckerman 1970, p. 19). Despite its limitations in both method of participation and participants (women, African-Americans, and, in some cases, nonlanded white men were excluded), the town meeting did allow for part of the citizenry to experience practical politics. Community problems were aired and resolved on the village green.

Jefferson, however, believed that town meetings or ward-republics were integral parts of community life in four ways: (1) to ensure the balance of power at home; (2) to preserve and encourage the public spirit of 1776; (3) to provide a general education for citizens; and (4) to maintain a public space for citizens to practice politics (Koch 1964, pp. 162–65). While all four functions provided a blueprint for Jefferson's view of communities and their roles, the fourth is most relevant to this discussion. Jefferson's idea of a space for practicing politics is best interpreted by Hannah Arendt. She saw both implications of this function: the actual creation of physical space for the daily practice of politics and Jefferson's often overlooked desire that each generation must create its own political community (Matthews 1984, p. 84).

Jefferson knew, however dimly, that the Revolution, while it had given freedom to the people, had failed to provide a space where freedom could be exercised. Only the representatives of the people, not the people themselves, had an opportunity to engage in those activities of "expressing, discussing, and deciding" [that] in a positive sense are the activities of freedom (Arendt 1965, p. 235).

Jefferson was the only one of the founders who recognized the need for a local meeting space (Mumford 1961). The political importance of the town meeting was lost on the founders and was "one of the tragic oversights of postrevolutionary political development" (p. 328).

The second portion of Jefferson's idea of a place to practice politics was his argument that every generation has a right to decide its own form of government. On its face, Jefferson's proposal of a new majority every 19 years sounds ludicrous and fraught with images of rebellion and tyranny. Arendt, however, defended Jefferson and realized the principle he was trying to establish: He did not want a radical change in government or even a revised Constitution; rather, he wanted a vehicle for the opinions of each generation to be heard and collective decisions made on how they should be governed (Arendt 1965, p. 123). Jefferson was opposed to the Constitution primarily because he believed that it would limit the powers of each new generation to decide the affairs of the political life themselves. He believed that each group of citizens should have the opportunity and power to begin anew (Matthews 1984, p. 84). Rousseau also warned of the dangers of too much representative democracy:

The English people think that it is free, but is greatly mistaken, for it is so only during the election of Members of Parliament; as soon as they are elected, it is enslaved and counts for nothing (1974, p. 161).

The circumstances of Ancient Greece and post-Revolutionary America lent themselves to more citizen-to-citizen interaction. Two elements of direct democracy must be understood, however. First is the idea that citizens must have a physical space to come together to decide the affairs of the community. This component of direct democracy has most to do with the logistics and practice of civic life. Second is the product of civic life, namely, action, and it is what Cronin addresses in *Direct Democracy* (1989). Cronin contends that the framers had from the outset planned an indirect democracy, but vestiges of a direct governance still must be acknowledged. The voices once heard on the town green are now transformed into actions like initiative, referendum, and recall. Still part of a representative system, these processes allow citizens direct input into governance and provide very tangible ways that citizens can participate directly in governing. In recent years, Governor Evan Mecham of Arizona was impeached just weeks before a scheduled recall. The well-publicized vote on Proposition 13 in June 1978 in California used initiative and referendum to cut property taxes (Cronin 1988, pp. 2–3).

While these processes diffuse power and give citizens more voice in public policy, they are only part of civic participation. The other component, which is much more difficult, is to participate prudently and wisely, using collective thinking and judgment. Direct democracy in America was never thus, but it was a deliberative process before action. In renewing American civic life, therefore, one must know not only the vehicles of access described by Cronin but also the enlargement of thinking that makes for wise public decisions.

The classical forms of direct democracy practiced by the Greeks in the *polis* and by the early Americans should be referenced metaphorically only. They are not models of citizenship that should be replicated. Rather, each provides background for understanding modern definitions of the rights, responsibilities, and obligations of an individual's relationship to government and fellow citizens, a background for citizenship (R. Brown 1986).

A discussion of early American public life without mention of the role of religious institutions is lacking.[1] While the purpose here is to sort out the participating origins of democracy, it must be acknowledged that the church has played a powerful role throughout history as both a moral supporter of and a challenger to the Constitution. Not surprisingly, attitudes vary greatly on the appropriate role that religion should play in public life. Separatists say keep the two separate and distinct. Social activists agree on separation but argue that the moral imperatives of the shared Judeo-Christian tradition mandate that religious institutions address critical issues in public life. Accommodationists believe that religion should be visible in public life and its symbols and that the church should be

---

1. For a complete discussion of religion in public life, see Bernstein 1986, Nauhaus 1984, and Reichley 1985.

actively involved in the moral life of civic society. And interventionists encourage direct political participation by the church and its leadership so as to influence the course of public life. The delicate balance that these views suggest concerned the founders. The basic question (then and now) of the appropriate involvement of religion in American public life is "whether a free society depends ultimately on religious values for cohesion and vindication of human rights" (Reichley 1985, pp. 3–5). While the answer and necessary preliminary discussion cannot be addressed here, we must recognize the overarching role that religion plays in defining who we are as a nation.

Thinking about New Definitions of Citizenship

After Alexis de Tocqueville visited America in 1831, he reminded the world of the importance of the civic relationship to citizenship:

> *Feelings and opinions are recruited, the heart [is] enlarged, and the human mind is developed only through the reciprocal relationship of men upon one another. I have shown that these influences are almost null in democratic countries; they must therefore be artificially created, and this can only be accomplished by associations. . . . If men are to remain civilized or to become so, the art of associating together must grow and improve in the same ratio in which the quality of the conditions increased* (1956, p. 200).

These "habits of the heart" speak only to part of the issue of citizenship. While an art or capacity of citizenship is evident, what is called for now is the science of citizenship—that is, the systematic study *and* practice of that peculiar and particular societal role.

Works written after World War I maintain the importance of civic associations and note that the central public problem of democracy is that it had not been tried (Follett 1920). Democracy was more than representative government and ballot boxes; it was rather a "genuine union of true individuals" where common ideas, purposes, and collective political will are developed. The true essence of democracy is creating vehicles for citizens where common goals can be defined and nurtured (Follett 1920).

The method for providing this vehicle for citizen participation, Follett suggests, is not through voting but through
organization of and association with groups. The organization
of people in small, local groups to address societal issues and
concerns is fundamental to a democracy. Within these kinds
of associations, the needs and will of each individual can
transcend private interests to produce an "all-will," a collective
political will. These associations allow citizens to learn "how
to associate" and to see the interdependence of their relationships with others in the community. Citizenship does not
mean singular participation, but pluralistic actions (Follett
1920). Acknowledging this interdependency of citizens and
groups is a basic premise of civic life, because it allows the
parties to see points of mutual interest. The individual citizen
comes to know himself better through the experience of citizenship (Sullivan 1982, p. 158).

Free Spaces (1986) explores models where people found
refuge together in places to think on their common interests,
highlighting the importance of these spaces for those citizens
to come together who had been excluded from or were on
the margins of political life. In particular, it explores early
labor organizations in America, African-American church life,
the populist farmers' movement, and women's voluntary
organizations.

> *Free spaces are settings between private lives and large-scale
> institutions where ordinary citizens can act with dignity,
> independence, and vision. [They] are, in the main, volun-
> tary forms of association with a relatively open and par-
> ticipatory character—many religious organizations, clubs,
> self-help, mutual aid societies, reform groups, neighborhood,
> civic, and ethnic groups, and a host of other associations
> grounded in the fabric of community life* (Boyte and Evans
> 1986, pp. 17–18).

The notion that voluntary associations are important to civic
life has support among neoconservatives. Some social critics
argue that these associations are obstacles to establishing total-
itarian regimes (Nisbet 1970); others hold that community
groups hedge the dangers of modern political life (Berger
1977). The traditional mediating units—family, church, neigh-
borhoods, and so on—provide a strong social defense. How-

ever supportive, the neoconservative view is fundamentally different from the communal "free space." Fundamental to the conservative view is that mediating organizations maintain order and stability through an ascribed "morality." The view that change and political upheaval can be healthy and useful in society threatens the social foundations they propose, and therefore, they believe, change itself could be unhealthy in this context. What is missing from their argument is how communities might be broad enough to facilitate productive social change. Boyte and Evans believe that this narrow view of community—maintaining the social order—"produces a political vision [that] contributes to the erosion of the very community institutions neoconservatives purport to support" (1986, pp. 185–86). Allowing citizens to associate and initiate change enhances public life (pp. 185–86).

Civic associations or public spaces can be found in every segment of society. Many opportunities, from churches to schools to volunteer organizations, support providing a space for public talk and action. Accordingly, these associations or institutions are usually thought to have a purpose that transcends individual interests. The important relationship that develops in these institutions that can be transferred to the broader public life is obligation. The reciprocity, affiliation, and bonding needed for association require consideration of a greater public purpose (D. Brown 1986, pp. 6–7). Societal institutions provide a place in which to practice obligation, both internally for the welfare of the associates and externally for the larger society. Involvement in voluntary institutions or public spaces gives citizens a place to practice politics through the development of shared values and purpose. Without such collective opportunities, citizenship can be very problematic:

> The expressions "keep your options open" [and] "you owe it to yourself" have turned obligation upside down. In a recent study, Robert Bellah and his colleagues see this as conduct of the "improvisational self," one who chooses values but is not necessarily bound by them. . . . Without institutional sanction, civic virtue is reduced to generous impulses, calculations of self-interest, or ideological statements. The members of the "new class" appear to be passionate consumers instead of active citizens (D. Brown 1986, pp. 8–9).

The Jeffersonian notion of citizenship underscored the importance of individuals' having a voice in the public affairs of the day. Jefferson believed that citizens were the ultimate power of society and brought to our political traditions the importance of having a public life. The concept that individuals who are productive in society have an integrated private and public life is a foundation necessary for building a new cadre of citizens. The American system of democracy, as it has evolved and partly as it is practiced today, is an alternative to an early repressive, monarchical system where decisions were made by a few for the many, an elite system that excluded large portions of Americans. Our political system today provides for participation by all Americans through a technological world that would be inconceivable to the founders.

Our increasingly technological and specialized world has lost the notion of the commonwealth (Boyte 1989). Commonwealth has two meanings: the self-governing community of equals where participation is the order of every day and the foundation of the life of the community that includes the resources and goods over which citizens have responsibility and authority. The concept of commonwealth, however, is finding new life. Communities throughout the nation are coming together on common issues. This renewal requires that citizens have access to all kinds of information and the skills to put such information to use. This knowledge and action are hinged on the capacity to make wise, collective decisions (Boyte 1989).

Today's world has many challenges to overcome (Brookfield 1987, pp. 52–54). Politically, the country has given way to mass representation in which most citizens are excluded from any level of direct decision making, a situation exacerbated by the issues themselves and by the actions of special interest groups and lobbyists that powerfully influence the public agenda. A problem endemic to American democracy today is the separation of citizens from policy makers as well as from each other. The media have contributed to the problem, as citizens come to see themselves as passive viewers and passive citizens.[2] This disconnection and passivity with public life cause individuals to isolate themselves more and

---

2. For further discussion on media and technology, see Murchland 1982 and 1983.

more. "They frequently turn inward, focusing exclusively on their private lives" (Brookfield 1987, p. 54).

Modern society is such, however, that the public and the private cannot be easily differentiated. Public decisions affect private lives every day. Defining the role of public life is crucial to understanding how the two concepts are inseparable and complementary.

The Public Discussion of Private Life

While we do not want to repeat the perils and inequities of the past, it is important to understand the balance between private responsibilities and public duties. As students leave academia to enter the work force or a graduate or professional school, they should take with them a concept of their "public" responsibilities. So often individuals delay participation until they are selected for the United Way's drive or the symphony committee. But the public self is forever with us; lives cannot be segmented. We perform public acts even if we never leave our homes.

Today, public participation has come to mean tradeoffs, special interests, elections, and power. The view that the political in our lives is narrow and confining has caused that all-too-frequent expression, "I'm staying out of politics; politics isn't for me." The reality is that all citizens are part of the political process, simply by driving on public roads or visiting a public park or attending a public university.

Dewey distinguished public and private by the nature or consequences of the act, not by who or what is involved. If the action is between two parties and either the conversation or resultant act does not go beyond them, then the activity is private. If, however, the consequences go beyond the two to affect the welfare of others, then it becomes public. This distinction has nothing to do with the concept of the individual versus the social. Private acts in this sense can certainly be social and serve the social good. Conversely, public acts are not necessarily socially useful; one of the most obvious public acts, for example, is waging war. "The line between public and private is drawn on the basis of the extent and scope of the consequences of acts that are so important as to need control, whether by inhibition or by promotion" (Dewey 1954, p. 15).

The distinction between public and private and the interrelationship of the two are difficult to discern. One reason is that citizens have lost the experiences that have allowed for distinctions between the private and the public, particularly the experience of a genuine public life (Arendt 1958, p. 28). "Public is almost synonymous with political, but political is not equated to governmental; instead, it concerns action in the community of peers." Neither a crowd of strangers at a movie nor the Department of Defense would qualify as a public (Arendt, cited in Pitkin 1981, p. 328).

We misunderstand public life if we equate it with politics, with the activities of government. Not only do we misunderstand it, we also strangle our sense of public possibilities. The heart of public life is simply the interaction of strangers and that is a basic and vital human experience, not a specialized political process (Palmer 1981, p. 22).

The reality of today's life is that public and private lives are irrevocably intertwined. No longer does the private life allow individuals to retreat. No matter what the level of active participation, every person is affected daily by "public" decisions. The Greek concept of man and *polis* as one and the same was replaced by the importance of the individual and the critical balance between the public and the private.

As individuals participate in public life, their powers not only add up but they multiply. And as people participate in public life, they are empowered in other ways as well. In particular, they gain confidence and competence in the skills required to function in public (Palmer 1981, p. 83).

The first picture of private that enters our minds is personal, intimate, within oneself, and that view is superimposed on a public image that is outgoing, separate, accessible, and open. Private and public spaces are described spatially (Sennett 1977, p. 16). Private means "in," public means "out," and one goes "out in public" when he is prepared to leave his personal space. The question is whether public and private refer to actual "places" or situations.

The often dim boundaries of the private and the public raise the question about where one ends and the other begins, however. An analysis of the importance of social science in developing a broader public imagination helps to frame the discussion about public and private (Mills 1959), address-

The reality of today's life is that public and private lives are irrevocably intertwined.

ing "the personal problems of milieu" and "the public issues of social structure" (p. 8). The implication is that public problems *stay* public until an individual is touched personally. The unemployment rate means more to the unemployed than to the employed; that is, how people see public problems has much to do with the context of their view. For citizens to create social change, they must begin to see personal issues in the public milieu (Mills 1959), but another observer believes Mills confuses the issue by referring to "personal trouble" as a private matter and an "issue" as a public matter, leaving the problem of perception unclear (for example, should unemployment be perceived as a personal problem or part of a widespread social condition?) (Pitkin 1981, p. 329). The following three-pronged definition helps clarify what might be included as part of public and private lives:

- *Public means access and attention.* Things that are public are accessible to all, visible. Terms like "public knowledge," "public opinion," and "out in public" are applications of this characteristic.
- *Public means its consequences have greater effects.* Something public affects a large number in its consequences and significance. It may not be recognized by those affected, however; for example, actions of a private corporation may have public impact and results. "Here the opposite of public is not secluded or withdrawn, but personal, of limited impact, affecting only select individuals or groups" (Pitkin 1981, p. 330), a reference to Mills's distinction between social condition and public issues. Issues become public when they become a focus of the public's attention.
- *Public means specific direction and control.* The public sphere is difficult to define in this way because of the multitude of factors that affect control. Pitkin referred to the publicness of government, public administration, and collective action. The quasi-public influence of multinational corporations, private industry, and the military-industrial complex blurs this characteristic; therefore, government control cannot be equated to public control (Pitkin 1981, pp. 329–30).

These defining elements bring the discussion back to Dewey, who contended that the idea of public or private is about the interaction, not the individuals involved. It further emphasizes the often blurry distinctions between what has been thought of as one or another. The example that government control is not public control raises the controversial issue of the role of the military-industrial complex in "governing" many facets of our lives. The point is that often very personal or private enterprise decisions have public implications. The same is true for most people. Their lives have a public dimension.

The move toward increasing individualism in American public life gives insight into the relationship between the public character and the nature of the political community. The kind of society created depends on the kind of people involved. Tocqueville's account of his visit to America examined the American character and analyzed how, through individuals, the wider political community could be sustained and flourish. Bellah and his colleagues in some respects retraced Tocqueville's visit by talking with citizens about their public and private lives and how those spheres relate to each other. They studied local politics, voluntary associations, families, churches, and political movements, all having private and public dimensions, and found anxiety about the complexion of the future among those interviewed. Although many resolved that America's charmed existence was eroding, they felt it could be reversed with the renewal of commitment and community (Bellah et al. 1985, pp. vii–ix). For all the lamentations about separateness and individualism in society, these authors drew a different conclusion:

> We have never been, and still are not, a collection of private individuals who, except for a conscious contract to create a minimal government, have nothing in common. Our lives make sense in a thousand different ways, most of which we are unaware of, because of traditions that are centuries, if not millennia, old. It is these traditions that help us know that it does make a difference who we are and how we treat one another (Bellah et al. 1985, p. 282).

The increasing withdrawal of citizens into their private domains and thoughts is "privatism" (Sullivan 1982). People are continually questioning the meaning of life and their place in it. "Part of the meaning of the current American retreat to privatism is a continuing search for what counts in life; a hunger orientation that neither the dynamics of capitalism growth nor the liberal vision of politics provides" (Sullivan

1982, p. 189). This current can be reversed only when it is acknowledged that the personal quest for a worthwhile life is interdependent with the larger world. "Large-scale social processes cannot remain merely technical issues but must be understood as part of the texture of personal living, just as personal life is woven into the patterns of collective organization" (pp. 159–60).

One of the places that these values of the democratic life are often found lacking is in the economic sphere. It is not a singular discussion of corporate citizenship or social responsibility; rather, it is about the values that a for-profit enterprise holds for its employees, customers, and competitors. It is not about "giving away the farm" but rather reflects democratic and civic principles throughout the economic system. If we are to recover these lost commitments to free institutions in a democratic society, economic life must have a public and democratic dimension (Sullivan 1982, p. 209). Organizations that operate on democracy in the work place and encourage quality circles and employees' involvement contain glimpses of this kind of civic response.

The clear message is that the idea of a collective life must pervade every aspect of society. The world is economically, socially, and politically intertwined, and its progress can come only through collective efforts.

The Political Life Today
The lives of citizens today are both private and public. Citizens have private responsibilities to perform at home, at work, at school, but most participate in the public either passively or actively each day.

> *The public life depends on regular encounters—most of them not overtly political—between strangers who cross each other's paths, become accustomed to each other's presence, and come to recognize their common claims on society. When the balance of life shifts heavily toward the private and these regular encounters diminish, people come into public only in moments of crisis. . . . The genuine public life is a continuous affair* (Palmer 1981, p. 84).

Public life is an activity that occurs outside and in conjunction with the private. Public becomes political when, by circumstances or by desire, individuals seek to define their common interests with others. What is encompassed in the political or public lives of citizens today?

Political life is not some leisure-time sport for aristocrats, in which they may cultivate their honor and display their powers. It is the activity through which relatively large and permanent groups settle how they will live together and decide their future to whatever extent that is within human power. Public life in this sense is of the utmost seriousness and importance, and potentially of surprising glory. But it never occurs in the abstract, without content; it always affects the lives of real people (Pitkin 1981, p. 343).

Politics and thus public life are about choices—usually difficult choices. The ability to make informed, rational decisions in concert with a community of fellow citizens provides the interconnectedness that is often lost in society. It is not an easy business. This notion of politics takes time to talk and reason through difficult options. The skills for participation are not a priori but must be learned for effective citizenship. A strong public life gives us the *potential* for decisions to be made by the community collectively, through participative action. What distinguishes politics from daily discourse is action on these decisions through "shared, collective, deliberate, active intervention in our fate, in what would otherwise be the by-product of private decisions" (Pitkin 1981, p. 344).

Because decisions about issues like foreign policy, environmental preservation, and social services affect the kind of collective life that is shared, public discussion and debate are critical. The interrelated consequences of choices must be understood. Those discussions of interdependency actually create a "public." "Public discussion aims to bring before the whole civic community an understanding of the 'externalities' of public choices. . . ," that is, what those choices will mean for various groups (Sullivan 1982, p. 166). This collective approach to public choices requires a different way of thinking.

To form public judgments, people have to spend considerable time assessing the interrelations of their many interests and the long-term consequences of their policy options. They have to reflect on their experiences and deliberate over choices. Being individually bright and logical is not enough (Mathews 1989, p. 49).

Politics, however, is not about consensus. Arendt insists that action occurs always among individuals who are diverse, whose ideas and endeavors collide and become entangled with one another (Canovan 1983, p. 301). The charge is for more politics in this sense, not less. The challenge is to "inform the discretion and enlarge the political experience of an active citizenry. . . a citizenry in action, capable of thinking as a 'we' in the name of public good" (Barber 1984, p. 135).

To understand the role and responsibilities of individuals living in a democracy is a primary step in fulfilling the office of citizenship. This understanding is predicated on how people learn or practice politics. The notion that "politics is good" if one candidate over another wins misses the fundamental principle of what a shared life is and can be. This political or civic life is not just about the "act" of choosing; it is concerned with the process by which citizens come to that choice and with whom. In part, it is about who is in the conversation.

Summary

Direct democracy is an ideal flawed with all kinds of pitfalls. The idea of re-creating the original democratic society that was marked by elitism, exclusion, and prejudice is unthinkable. But the further realization is frightening that, as a representative democracy, almost no opportunity exists to think and act together as a nation. The task then is not to re-create a flawed past; it is rather to imagine a new civic system that allows for modern society to move beyond special interests and partisan politics and to raise the expectations of ourselves and each other. Jefferson warned that each generation of citizens must be allowed to determine its own society or it would be chained to the past. As he said in a letter to James Madison, "The earth belongs always to the living generation" (Matthews 1984, p. 22). While the Constitution provides the basis of governance, each generation in fact has control over the way it will govern itself. Each age can, in some sense, think anew.

Citizens must feel that they do indeed hold office in the country; with that sense of belonging to the whole come the responsibility and right to participate in the public realm. The office of citizenship still requires an informed, educated citizenry with the necessary skills to participate. The challenge for higher education is to find a way to meet that need.

Education, since its beginning in this country, has been a source of social vision and values for Americans (Sloan 1977, pp. 163–65). Jefferson's enlightened citizenry mirrored the nation's belief in the power of education in building a national community and purpose. But Jefferson's ideas went beyond the three Rs; he called for citizens who could understand and act on the important issues of the day. Education was called upon to help develop the skills to participate.

Finally, this office of citizen was built on the ideal that the citizen as ruler is disinterested in narrow interests and instead is concerned with the welfare of the whole—and asks continually, "What is the collective good for the nation or the community?" Answering this question requires a sense of "obligation," "responsibility," "duty," and "judgment" rather than singular, individual perspectives. Simply put:

> *The public and civic virtue required of the responsible citizen is, after all, a moral quality, a posture not quantifiable in terms of truth expended or amount of information accumulated* (Ketcham 1987, p. 163).

Citizenship does not mean mastering all the facts or having answers to all the questions. Rather, it means that when one assumes the role of citizen, "I" becomes "we." Understanding this personal and civic transformation goes way beyond the narrow view of citizens as "private agents pursuing private interests in the political marketplace" (Barber 1988, pp. 200–201). The civic role suggested here is interactive, collective, and mutualistic. Citizenship is not about one person; it is about all people.

Reminiscences of the public life of the Ancient Greeks raise a question about how that existence might be played out every day, and the response puts the discussion and the issues at hand into a human perspective. Ideally, the *polis* was:

> . . . *small enough so that each person would know his neighbor and could play a part in the governance of the city, large enough so that the city could feed itself and defend itself; a place of intimate bonding in which the private sphere of the home and family and the public sphere of civic democracy would be but one easy step apart* . . . (Ignatieff 1984, p. 107).

HIGHER EDUCATION'S ROLE IN CIVIC EDUCATION

From its beginnings, higher education has played a significant role in shaping American society. Its early purpose was to prepare an elite group of the nation's men for service in the secular and religious life of the new nation. Early, however, American institutions expanded this tradition by introducing to their mission the idea of serving the social needs of the nation. In America, higher education was seen as the means for providing manpower and knowledge for the new country (Bok 1982, pp. 51–62). The British educator, Sir Eric Ashby, said, "The great American contribution to higher education has been to dismantle the walls around the campus" (Bok 1982, p. 65). The first American college—Harvard, founded in 1636—had a clear social dimension: to train literate clergy, to educate lawyers and the New World's leadership, and to advance humanistic traditions in the country. As more institutions were established, their societal goals also became clear. In addition to promoting traditional liberal arts education, colleges and universities had the charge "to instill in their students piety, loyalty, and responsible citizenship—and to transmit knowledge that would be useful for the practical demands of the emerging nations" (Boyer and Hechinger 1981, p. 9).

These early colleges and universities were seen as unifiers for the goals of the larger society. They performed this role in three basic ways:

1. promoting a common American culture;
2. teaching moral philosophy within the institution that, among other purposes, was to integrate various disciplines and to serve as an ethic guide for students; and
3. producing leaders for America that were to be, in Jefferson's words, an "aristocracy of talent and virtue" (Sloan 1977, pp. 165–66).

The early American colleges upheld the English tradition of the liberal arts curriculum but were more concerned with character development than the unearthing of new knowledge. They believed that classical education, taught in a residential environment, was very important for student development, what Cotton Mather called "the collegiate way of living." Colleges and universities were educating a small group of men for community leadership and providing the country with the elite, educated citizenry it needed (Brubaker and Rudy 1976, p. 23). Even before the adoption of the Constitution, many educators tried to emphasize preparation for broader civic participation over narrow religious goals. In the mid-18th century, William Livingston at Kings College and Benjamin Franklin and William Smith at the College at Philadelphia argued for a civic mission (Butts 1982, p. 380). As early as 1818, with Thomas Jefferson's Rockfish Gap Commission, a vision existed of education for the common good (Miller 1988, pp. 9–10). This work had begun for Jefferson in 1779 when he proposed the study of the civic arts at the College of William and Mary.

The Rockfish Gap Commission, appointed to select the site for the University of Virginia, outlined these purposes for higher education:

> *To expound the principles and structures of government. . . . To harmonize and promote the interests of agriculture, manufacturing, and commerce. . . . To enlighten them with mathematical and physical sciences. . . . And generally to form them to habits of reflection and correct action* (Rockfish Gap Commission 1961, pp. 194–95).

As society changed in the late 19th and early 20th centuries, however, so did higher education. With the industrial revolution and urbanization, disciplinary definitions and divisions became more pronounced and the notion of a unified intellectual and cultural world seemed to diminish. While the vision of higher education as a promoter and instructor of civic values was not lost, it became clear that the approach would have to change (Sloan 1977, p. 166).

When Alexis de Tocqueville visited America in 1831, he observed that America had few ignorant and few especially learned. The nation's emphasis was on primary education; the push for higher education had not yet begun. Tocqueville's visit, however, was on the eve of a major metamorphosis in higher education in the United States, which would make it much more accessible to the larger citizenry. With this change came a growing debate about higher education's purposes. The traditionalists felt that knowledge was an end in itself, while the opposition was more pragmatic and saw that the role of higher education was to prepare Americans for a profession. Inherent in all the debate, however, was another controversy: the responsibility of higher education to educate for citizenship.

For many Americans, education for citizenship was viewed as a central role of kindergarten through grade 12, not higher education. Jefferson and the other founders had assigned the task of preparing an educated citizenry to the nation's burgeoning system of primary and secondary education. In addition to the three Rs, precollegiate education was to instill in its charges the values of equality under the law and limited government. "The model citizen of early republican theory knew what his rights were and defended them from infringement by his fellow citizens and the State" (Lasch 1978, p. 130). Early "civic" education stressed ancient and modern history particularly so that, in Jefferson's words, students might be able to judge "the actions and designs of men, to know ambition under every disguise it may assume—and knowing it, to defeat its views" (p. 151).

This view of civic education assumed that if students were exposed to certain scenarios of history, responsible citizenship was a logical conclusion. The few students who went on to higher education were grounded in the practical knowledge needed for citizenship, but the larger issues of access and public-spiritedness were assumed. Higher education was not the beginning of education for citizenship but, to most people's mind, the end.

Unfortunately, this civic foundation that higher education counted on from its entering students was eroding. The preparation for citizenship was no longer seen as a deliberate purpose of the public schools. A study for the Education Commission of the States in 1979 offers one explanation:

> Originally, in the public school concept, citizenship education was the primary focus of all education; by the mid-19th century, it had become identified with the social studies—particularly the civics class—and thus was treated more and more as a special area of study, or a "course," rather than a total school purpose. Then after Sputnik came a high emphasis on scientific methods, with resultant reduction of interest in the socialization process. Even social scientists felt that "citizenship" was not an intellectually worthy goal of education. During the same period, the trend toward electives as well as a general broadening introduced many competing subjects and courses. Thus, from being an overall priority concern, citizenship education was gradually relegated to a single discipline—a few courses—and

then those courses were submerged in the proliferation of interests and concerns taken on by the school (Reische 1987, p. 15).

This analysis is relevant to higher education's civic role in two ways: (1) The hypothesis is that students come to higher education less prepared for responsible citizenship than previously, and (2) the decline in the emphasis on civic preparation by the public schools has paralleled the decline in higher education. No longer does a conscious effort exist to meet the educational goal of educating for citizenship at any educational level.

The opposition to a specific civic component in the curriculum and the more practical and scientific courses of study has a fierce tradition in higher education, however. The Yale Faculty Report of 1828 was the bulwark defense of the classic curriculum. The Yale faculty accepted the notion that America needed larger numbers of citizens with higher education but believed that it could best be accomplished by a homogeneous citizenry with a common core education (Miller 1988, pp. 12–13). By the late 19th and early 20th centuries, higher education began to expand its offerings and its availability to larger numbers of Americans. Part of this response was the elective system.

In *The American College* (1908), Alexander Flexner called for a redefinition of the purpose of higher education, specifically connecting the individual with life. He especially criticized the elective system, because, he believed, it did not represent a purpose or structure for institutions. American colleges, from their foundings, prepared "men" for specific professions—namely, the church, the law, or gentleman farming. What had evolved at that time, in Flexner's opinion, was not only the specific curricular offerings but "a rejection of the limiting of the social positions and functions [that] knowledge and learning supported and defined." The elective system, however, was not a remedy to the problem. Rather, Flexner thought of it as fragmented and unorganized. The alternative he advocated included some electives, but the overall direction gave a wholeness to the parts.

It is no foregone conclusion that mere existence within a community will effectively prepare a man for his proper part in its intellectual interests and social struggles. I hold

*that if liberal education is anything more than a personal
indulgence or a personal opportunity, the college has a very
distinct task in reference to the impersonal aspects of social
and civic life* (Flexner, cited in Wegener 1978, p. 57).

One of Flexner's contemporaries was William Raney Harper,
president of the University of Chicago. Harper saw the broad-
ening role and contributions of higher education. He contended that the role of universities was not ornamental but
that they were vehicles for the transformation and enrichment
of American lives. The move from the private world to the
public world meant more accessibility and more contributions
to economic and technological growth. What had been lost
is the emphasis on the individual contribution to the civic
enterprise. The original role of preparing the student for a
profession was only part of an institution's mission. Actually,
the preparation for participation in a democratic society was
the goal. As higher education moved away from concentrating
on the individual to examining the collective purposes, the
ideal of preparing responsible citizens became a rhetorical
assumption (Wegener 1978, pp. 30–37).

A tangential but important evolution occurred in 1862 with
the Morrill Act and the birth of public service initiatives. The
public service movement linked the "ivory tower" to the
"town square" but was not synonymous with the earlier
emphases on preparation for citizenship. Campus outreach,
extension, and adult education might have involved students
but were not seen as a part of civic education (Bok 1982, pp.
62–63).

In the 20th century, higher education redefined its mission
beyond the classic curriculum and public service. Two primary
themes emerged: (1) The notion of an "expert" was popularized and has, to some extent, replaced the goal of a generally educated person, and (2) greater access to higher education for all Americans, regardless of race or gender, was seen
as a way to protect and enhance the democratic goals of life,
liberty, and the pursuit of happiness. Education at all levels
became more defined and prescribed. With that clarity, the
social goals of education were confirmed (Sloan 1977, p. 167).

Both these themes—developing experts and providing
access—have profoundly affected the nation. The mind-
boggling advancements of science and technology (and at
times their unwanted results) have required that almost every

profession, from engineering to teaching, develop increasingly minute areas of expertise. As to the question of access, little doubt exists that the integration of America's white institutions in the late fifties and sixties had a symbiotic effect on the integration of society at large. George Wallace's "stand in the schoolhouse door" at the University of Alabama and less dramatic instances at other institutions to prevent African-Americans from entering higher education seem farther away than 25 years. *Brown* v. *Board of Education* said to all educational institutions that equality in admissions must be provided. Yet with both of these areas contributing greatly to the economic and social development of the country, American institutions had no unified statement about their very critical role in preparing citizens for leadership of an increasingly diverse and complex nation.

Another phenomenon was occurring—the birth of community and junior colleges. The marriage of college and community has had a natural home over the years. The community and junior college movement that emerged after World War II was in part intended to bridge the gap between town and gown and make education accessible. The community college was a natural affinity and historical mandate to "practice" community. "The community college can be an effective convener, a valuable forum, a meeting ground where the common good is discussed" (Gardner 1987). While other kinds of institutions also provide that kind of connection to the community, community colleges and their students offer a great opportunity to serve as models for a democratic community. The American Association of Community and Junior Colleges has adapted development of citizenship as a major goal of its membership.

All institutions, including higher education, that are defined as vital to the commonwealth might be termed "civic institutions" (Stanley 1989) for two reasons: (1) the ethos of democracy, such that it emphasizes the transformation of all political subjects into participating citizens, and (2) the interdependence of the world under the impetus of science, technology, and commerce. The point echoes the sentiment of the higher education community that it was only one of the institutions responsible for civic development. The demands in scholarship and research brought on by the technological explosion became a more pressing priority. Colleges and universities hold the ticket to the country's survival in two critical ways: (1) Higher education can be extremely valuable in helping economies at all levels be competitive in the international environment, and (2) higher education can educate bright, capable technocrats and professionals but also educate people who will be well-rounded competent citizens (Peirce 1988, p. 9). Unless colleges and universities can do both things while providing practical expertise and leadership day to day, we will be a country at risk in the future. Universities do well what they are chartered to do—provide education—but they must also help students synthesize that knowledge in a larger, social context (p. 14).

While most college catalogs have always included the rhetoric of continuing interest in civic development for students, practice is another matter. A study by the Carnegie Commission on Higher Education found that administrators and faculty surveyed felt their institution placed preparation for citizenship at 25 of 47 goals—and development of students' character at 41. When asked what goals the institution *should* strive for, the same group placed preparation for citizenship at 15 and character development at 16 (Gross and Gambsch 1974, pp. 46–47). While no one on campus deliberates about what that means pedagogically, the goals remain that a college education should prepare an individual for the civic life:

> *For all the nagging doubts of the contemporary age, the belief persists that the process most capable of holding the intellectual center of society together, preventing it from disintegrating into unconnected splinters, is education. It may not have lived up to this vision of cohesion, but, at its best, the campus is expected to bring together the views and experiences of all its points and create something greater than the sum, offering the prospect that personal values will be clarified and the channels of our common life will be deepened and renewed* (Boyer and Hechinger 1981, p. 56).

What these writers allude to is a rebirth of the civic purposes of education. In fact, this theme has had a long shelf life and has found its way into conversations about cultural foundations, general education, liberal arts, professional education, community or public service, citizenship education, service or experiential learning, or what, in Arendt's definition, might be termed political or civic education.

It is not at all clear, however, what the civic dimensions of education should be or how they should be integrated into the overall educational program. If students were born citizens, there would be no need to teach them civic responsibility (Barber 1989). Likewise, if students were born literate, there would be no need to teach them literature (p. 67). A number of arguments have been put forth, however, that contend that citizenship will come with education in and of itself. The dilemma for higher education is to examine its role in preparing students to assume their civic roles, given a changing world that is becoming even more complex.

Citizens are needed not in thousands, but in millions, who can contribute to the solution of massive public problems brought on by a fragmented, technological society. The desired civic society is inclusive; it shares common perspectives and has opportunities for citizens to express *their* will and the *all*-will toward higher civic purposes. Students prepared for citizenship must have an understanding of the political system as well as a sense of shared values, practical wisdom, and the skills to discuss, judge, and act with their fellow citizens on public policy issues of the day. The struggle is balancing individual and community needs (Boyer 1988).

Ways to Prepare Students for Citizenship

The writing, research, and opinions on ways that the undergraduate curriculum fulfills its responsibility to prepare students for responsible citizenship have run the gamut over the years. No one way exists, however, and to frame the debate, this discussion uses six general categories: (1) cultural traditions and classical education; (2) community and public service and experiential education; (3) studies of leadership; (4) general and liberal arts education; (5) civic or public leadership education; and (6) the catch-all—other. These categories are focused primarily on undergraduate education. While they are not clear-cut interpretations or exclusive categories, they do illustrate the span of opinion on how higher education meets its educational goals.

Cultural traditions and classical education

This category represents a group of thinkers who believe that classical education is an end to itself. Articulated by Cardinal Newman in *The Idea of the University* during the mid-19th century, the idea was supported later by Mortimer Adler and Robert Hutchins. "Liberal education, viewed in itself, is simply the cultivation of the intellect as such, and its object is nothing more nor less than intellectual" (Newman, cited in Brubaker 1977, p. 70). Adler expanded this notion of cultivating an intellect, believing that liberal education was relevant to all people at all points in history. And this "common" dimension is what Hutchins believed was the purpose of the liberal arts—said another way, the purpose of education. This proclivity for liberal study has been most vividly expressed by the "great books" curriculum. Hutchins believed that the basic requirement for the formation of a political community was a common liberal education. The liberal arts were to him the arts of communication and using the mind (Brubaker 1977, pp. 70–72).

Current advocates of the "great books" and common knowledge genre believe that the nation and the world must have a common base of knowledge on which to operate. Many believe that a need exists to build a common core of knowledge that would strengthen our ability to act in a unified way. An argument for a cultural literacy holds that it is far more than skill; cultural literacy demands the mastery of large quantities of information and facts (Hirsch 1987, pp. 2, 108). It requires that citizens be able to read and comprehend any writing addressed to the general public. The arguments are built in part on the Ciceronian and Jeffersonian notion of an educated, informed citizenry: that citizens should be able to discuss economic issues, moral dilemmas, technological changes, and the most arcane specialties. If not, society is in danger of being intimidated by experts and advancing technology.

The more specialized and technical our civilization becomes, the harder it is for nonspecialists to participate in the decisions that deeply affect their lives. If we do not achieve a literate society, the technicians, with their arcane specialties, will not be able to communicate with us nor we with them (Hirsch 1987, p. 31).

This idea of a common core of understanding and universal public discourse is a way of enabling all citizens to participate in the political process. The dangers of modern relativism or historicism in American higher education and the loss of values threaten to "close the minds" of American college students (Bloom 1987). The problem in American higher education is that it has lost its capacity to influence the development of citizenship by having no clear purpose or direction. Historicism—the belief that individuals are conditioned (and, in most cases, unduly) by their cultural surroundings—is the problem that has and will greatly affect society. Americans, especially today's students, no longer think or believe that Truths exist but that only manufactured life-styles and values exist. Rather than labeling any as racist or ethnocentric, they treat values of all cultures as equal and important. Instead of liberating us, Bloom says, this kind of valueless thinking has caused people to close their minds to the notion of a true understanding of the Good and accept a potpourri of values. The move by radicals in the 60s to open campuses that resulted in ethnic studies, women's studies, internships, and service learning has, in this analysis, closed academic life to the search for the ultimate Good and Beautiful (Bloom 1987).

Educational systems have goals about the kind of human being they want to produce. All political regimes need citizens who follow and support their fundamental principles. Thus, our American educational system produces individuals who support democratic values, tasks, and character that undergird the egalitarian notion of democracy. In the early days of the republic, the country wanted people who knew the rights doctrine, understood the Constitution, and studied the history of our founding principles. "A powerful attachment to the letter and the spirit of the Declaration of Independence gently conveyed, appealing to each man's reason, was the goal of the education of democratic man" (Bloom 1987, p. 26).

This kind of education differed greatly from the traditional communities built on myth, passion, and authoritarianism that produced fanatical patriots. According to Bloom, the difference between the two had to do with what it means to be an American. The old view of education for the democratic man recognized and accepted the natural rights of man and the bases of unity and sameness that went with those fundamentals. The new kind of education for the democratic personality disregards natural rights or historical origins in favor of complete openness. This educational philosophy emphasizes that the natural right theory and historical origins are flawed and regressive.

There is no enemy other than the man who is not open to everything. But when there are no shared goals or vision of the public good, is the social contract any longer possible?

. . . Relativism has extinguished the real motive of education, the search for a good life. . . . No longer is there hope that there are great wise men in other places and times who can reveal the truth about life except for the few remaining young people who look for a quick fix from a guru. Gone is the real historical sense of a Machiavelli, who wrested a few hours from each busy day in which "to don regal and courtly garments, enter the courts of the ancients, and speak with them" (Bloom 1987, pp. 27, 34–35).

Bloom represents a group of classical educators who believe that to produce the kind of people needed for a democratic society, the Great Books and classical thinkers must be returned to the curriculum, contending that the study of ancient and classical works may require "creative" misinterpretation to be able to identify the Truth. His argument, and the one proposed to a lesser extent by Hirsch, is that we need a common language or culture to be a functional society. The diversity and pluralism that many espouse in fact prevents us from identifying, understanding, and promoting our commonness. These advocates said that higher education is failing by not helping students move beyond their limited spheres to an understanding of the universal values on which we, as a country, should operate.

The issue of liberal education teaching values has raised hackles. The debate about rational versus moral education is not a new one. The Greeks asked whether virtue can be taught (Hocking, cited in Brubaker 1977, p. 73). Without reopening this argument, we can note the controversy about the appropriateness and effectiveness of teaching *about* something (facts) or teaching *for* something (behavior). For the Greeks, the issue was whether one could learn virtue and morals from learning about them apart from practice and commitment (Brubaker 1977, p. 73). This argument is also part of the debate about civic education. It supports the contention that teaching *about* citizenship through history, literature, biography, and so on fulfills the institution's role to educate for citizenship—that reading the classics, developing a core of knowledge, and understanding the common fabric of history promote the civic building blocks.

The "great books debate" is part of a broad-based movement called "canon formation," which is the generic name for those who question how and why the classics became the classics and their relevancy to today's students. The inherent criticism in the classics or common learning approach centers around *whose* common learning we should teach. In fact, an anthology, *Multicultural Literacy: Opening of the American Mind* (1988) seeks to expose the narrowness of both Bloom and Hirsch. As for Hirsch, he is right as far as he goes, but much more in our collective cultures should be included. The editors say of them: "Both writers seem to think that most of what constitutes contemporary American and world culture was immaculately conceived by a few men in Greece around 900 B.C., came to its full expression in Europe a few centuries later, and began to decline around the middle of the 19th century" (Simonson and Walker 1988, p. xvi). Many feminist scholars and ethnic and racial groups agree with this perspective and are emphatic about the racial, gender, and class biases of the classics.

The central argument of the classics is curricular and questions the legitimacy of what is taught in preparing students for lifelong participation. In summary, the classics argument says that the reason for reading the classics (or having a clear, historical perspective) is to broaden experience and move students beyond their own lives. "Precisely the 'irrelevance' of the classics is what makes them relevant" (Howe 1988, pp. 478–79).

Community and public service and experiential education

A plethora of writing and work in this area supports including community service as part of the undergraduate experience.[3] Practiced partially in the form of apprentices and then later in the medical professions, the concept of "service-learning" as part of the curriculum has academic acceptance for undergraduate students in the last 20 years. The Southern Regional Education Board (SREB) began one of the most comprehensive programs in 1967. Using work from the Newman Task Force and the Carnegie Commission on Higher Education Studies, SREB organized a regionwide service-learning internship program with 15 southern states. Uniting with individual colleges and universities, the program formalized the use of service-learning and launched nationwide attention on it as

---

3. An excellent compendium on the subject is *Combining Service and Learning: A Resource Book for Community and Public Service* (NSIEE 1990).

a pedagogical device. Even in the early days, the internships were geared to a student's interests and major, and a discussion component included time for the student and faculty sponsor to reflect on the experience (SREB 1973).

The significant contributions of SREB and other related groups have given rise to this new movement in higher education. The National Society for Internships and Experiential Education, for example, has worked for over 15 years with faculty and administrators to think more systemically and pedagogically about ways that experiential learning can relate classroom theory to a community problem or situation. In 1985, another group was started. Dr. Frank Newman, president of the Education Commission of the States, Dr. Donald Kennedy of Stanford University, and Father Timothy Healy, then president of Georgetown University, formed the Campus Compact Project for Public and Community Service as a national clearinghouse for university-sponsored public service activities (Campus Compact 1988, p. 73). Housed at Brown University, the Compact now numbers more than 140 college and university presidents as members. Similarly, state organizations like the Pennsylvania Association of Colleges and Universities initiated a statewide Pennsylvania Compact. Joining the ranks in recent years have been student-generated voluntary groups, one of the best known of which is the Campus Outreach Opportunity League (COOL), founded in 1984 by Wayne Meisel, then a recent graduate of Harvard, and a colleague, Bobby Hackett. They traveled to colleges and universities across the country, helping them establish volunteer programs. Now with over 350 campuses participating, COOL's leadership addresses the match of volunteers with local needs (Moskos 1988, p. 113). "Contrary to the popular myth of student apathy toward public service, there is a very real sense of responsibility and yearning to service, and we are only beginning to tap it" (Kennedy 1988). Building on the idea supported by John Dewey and others that theory needs experience, many educators contend that exposure to service opportunities will broaden the student's view of the world and enable him to have a practical experience in solving problems. "The school cannot be a preparation for social life except as it reproduces, within itself, typical conditions of social life" (Dewey 1909, p. 14).

For years, most institutions have had some kind of internship program. Programs like the Phillips Brooks House at Har-

Contrary to the popular myth of student apathy ... there is a very real sense of responsibility and yearning to service.

vard, in existence since 1894, place students in volunteer situations. They are joined now by such programs as the Center for Public Service at Brown University, the Center for Public Service at Stanford, and others. A few have made it a visible part of the academic program. Antioch College in Yellow Springs, Ohio, requires that all students have work experiences along with their classroom work. Berea College (Kentucky), Warren Wilson College (North Carolina), and Berry College (Georgia) require their students to work on campus to help defray costs (while it is not always the same as service-learning per se, it is out of the same tradition). Other institutions have made service a required part of the curriculum.

Alverno College in Milwaukee has an outcome-oriented curriculum requiring proficiencies in eight competencies, one of which is effective citizenship. Effective citizenship has four levels. Levels one and two focus on developing students' understanding of contemporary issues and helping them realize their place in the larger world. Sequential courses in these levels are drawn from social sciences, arts, humanities, sciences, and psychology. The remaining two required levels are experiential, and students work in the community. The learning themes for students include commitment to a better life for all, recognition of diversity, and improved relationships between members of the community (Hutchings and Wutzdorff 1988, pp. 9–10). Wittenberg College in Springfield, Ohio, requires that all of its sophomore students perform 30 hours of community service. Finally, Rutgers University in 1989 approved a program that may eventually result in a requirement for each student to complete a course in civic responsibility, citizen education, and community service that includes community service as one of the experiential learning projects required and addresses the key concepts of a political community, the meaning of citizenship, and other areas like diversity, service, leadership, public and private interests, and the broader notion of community. In his commencement address in May 1988, the late President Edward J. Blaustein set the stage for this new initiative:

Making service to others a requirement of the undergraduate liberal arts degree . . . [not only helps students] serve usefully as citizens of a democracy . . . [but may also help combat] racism, sexism, homophobia, religious intolerance, and fear and animosity toward foreigners [as well as] pro-

viding an alternative to the naked pursuit of individual interest and material gain (Rutgers University 1989, p. 17).

The program began in fall 1989 and will be phased in over the next few years.

These examples are not an inclusive list. They do, however, demonstrate clearly that service-learning is being recognized as an integral part of learning, and of civic learning in particular.

In the current literature, the return of practice or service has taken many different forms. The issue of national service is a highly visible element on the governmental agenda. This concept stresses the involvement of all Americans in the activities of their communities as volunteers. Public service has taken two different roads. The first is synonymous with community service or service-learning, that is, encouraging younger citizens to engage in internships, practicums, or voluntary assistance with community agencies and public sector organizations. These activities are for credit or not for credit and can be done in a variety of times. (An estimated 15 to 25 percent of students regularly engage in some type of service activity [Toufexis 1987].) The second concept of public service relates to government service and the quality of the people recruited for that service; the participation is designated service work that is required by the federal or state governments (Moskos 1988). For this discussion, the issue is not service in and of itself but the public dimension or participatory nature of that service.

No convincing evidence suggests that most institutions have given much attention to "the civic learning associated with maintaining and improving the fundamental civic ideas and values of the democratic political community" (Carnegie Commission 1973). As late as 1973, little copy was given to the civic purposes of higher education. In the evaluation of the five purposes of education, Commission members viewed the goal of "general education for citizenship" as "most uneven, most controversial, and most in need of clarification" (p. 388).

The situation is changing, however. As community service becomes more prevalent, institutions question how service could or should fit into curricula as part of civic preparation. At the Educational Summit in September 1989 held at the University of Virginia, UVa President Robert O'Neil was asked about the greatest weakness of incoming UVa students. He replied that although students come to the university well prepared academically, his greatest disappointment was that students do not seem to have a commitment to public or community service—and that he wished the university could do more about that. Some action is apparent in that direction, however. "One cannot learn civic responsibility or public leadership by taking a class. . . . We must think about what it is that students can actually do that will give them the hands-on experience of being a leader in the best sense of that term, and of understanding their relationships in a broader sense than just self-interest" (Newman 1985, p. 10).

The experiential approach to civic education allows students to see firsthand how organizations and communities go about their work. The approach to community service or other types of experiential learning varies from institution to institution and individual to individual, but it is intended to allow students educational exposure and observation on the one hand and, more important, an opportunity to apply the theory they have learned to a real problem or situation. The role of experiential education in citizenship education is to help the student participate in politics and derive meaning from those experiences (Chiarelott 1979, p. 82).

Service-based education needs caution, however, and two fundamental principles must be observed:

1. The service provided must be competent. *If community service is to have any real social relevance—be, in fact, more then a dilettante tinkering with irritants to the middle-class conscience—it will be affecting people's lives in a fundamental way. . . . For example, students are transient, and service, which demands sustained attention over a period of time, may simply not be possible.*

2. The service must include reciprocity. *There are two dangers beyond "do-goodery" [that] must be avoided. The first is that of "academic voyeurism." . . . The cynical use of other people's miseries for academic data is only morally, not functionally, more reprehensible than dilettante dithering for genuine reasons of social concern. . . . The second danger is the converse—that students may be exploited. Students may be used as anything from cheap labor to political pawns. . . . The prin-*

ciple of reciprocity demands that each party to a social service arrangement has something worthwhile to gain from it (Goodlad 1975, pp. 20–21).

Table 1 is a list of good practices for service-learning prepared by the Johnson Foundation in Racine, Wisconsin, and 50 other organizations to create a set of good practices for combining service and learning.

TABLE 1

PRINCIPLES OF GOOD PRACTICE FOR SERVICE-LEARNING

An effective service program:
* Engages people in responsible and challenging actions for the common good;
* Provides structured opportunities for people to reflect critically on their service experience;
* Articulates clear service and learning goals for everyone involved;
* Allows for those with needs to define those needs;
* Clarifies the responsibilities of each person and organization involved;
* Matches service providers and service needs through a process that recognizes changing circumstances;
* Expects genuine, active, and sustained organizational commitment;
* Includes training, supervision, monitoring, support, recognition, and evaluation to meet service and learning goals;
* Ensures that the time commitment for service and learning is flexible, appropriate, and in the best interests of all involved; and
* Is committed to program participation by and with diverse populations.

Source: Porter-Honnett and Poulsen 1989.

The attention given to university-based efforts parallels the national scene. The efforts by the president and the Congress to have a "national service program" have drawn both emphasis and dollars to the service issue.[4] Building on William James's call for a "moral equivalent to war," the civilian service movement contends that younger people, older people, and those in between can both contribute to and benefit from sustained national service. Introduced in 18 forms to the Congress, the bills call for legislation that will generate 1 billion

---

4. For a complete treatment of the history and specifics of this initiative, see Moskos 1988.

hours of community service over five years using a variety of approaches.

The proposed campus-based portion of the National Service Bill expands the Innovative Projects for Community Services and Student Financial Independence Program administered by the Fund for the Improvement of Post-Secondary Education; provides increased incentive for higher education institutions to use work-study funds for community service-learning programs; creates a 50 percent set-aside for community service in State Student Incentive Grant Programs for funds appropriated above $75 million; and allows partial cancellation of loans in Perkins and Stafford loan programs for persons performing full-time community service (AACJC 1989).

The country has seen the value of the service component throughout its history. Recent examples, such as the Civilian Conservation Corps, the National Youth Administration, and, more recently, the Peace Corps, VISTA, and University Year for Action have all shown that service programs have accomplished something for society, provided personal enrichment for the participants, and emphasized the ideal of public service in the younger generation. Many other national groups are not included in this summary. In a related effort, the National Commission on Public Service concentrates on how to improve and expand the corps of *public* servants for the government. Other organizations—the Washington Internship Program, Democratic Leadership Council, Volunteer, The National Center, Youth Policy Institute, Access Unlimited—have significantly contributed to the conversation about service. "By providing opportunities to perform service, as educators, we are encouraging in our students a lifelong commitment to social concerns and active citizenship" (Newman, Milton, and Stroud 1985, p. 9).

An ideal service program would include both students and faculty. It would help students move beyond themselves and be a way "to get some kind of moral assistance" with students who are interested only in their personal gain (Coles 1989b, pp. 20–21).

Studies of leadership
The study of leadership has stimulated new interest in the last few decades. Former Health, Education, and Welfare Secretary John Gardner's 12-volume monograph on leadership sponsored by the Independent Sector (1987) joins a myriad

of work done by the private sector. These efforts have placed the issue on the forefront on campuses and in corporate board rooms. Initiatives include courses to programs to summer institutes designed for the emerging leader. Leadership America, a Dallas-based operation, hosts 100 college and university students each summer in an intensive program that includes a variety of techniques and approaches to leadership. Duke University's Leadership Program offers courses and does research on the general topic of leadership. The University of Richmond's new Jepson Center was endowed to study leadership and create an undergraduate major. The Humphrey Institute at the University of Minnesota has programs in reflective and intuitive leadership. An innovative new thrust has been launched by the Class of '55 at Princeton University, which is trying to establish the Center for Civic Leadership at Princeton to reengage alumni in civic participation and service. The list goes on. Advocates of leadership say that awakening the next generation of leaders for the country means creating vehicles for teaching the topic directly and, in some cases, self-selecting those that look most promising.

With a grant from the Henry Luce Foundation, the Council for Liberal Learning at the Association of American Colleges spent considerable time studying leadership programs on campus. The study identified three primary categories for leadership programs:

1. The cocurricular leadership development program arising out of a student development office or direct student initiative;
2. The academic course that draws mainly on the literature of social psychological and management studies; and
3. The liberal arts academic course that places the study of leadership in the context of both the humanities and the social sciences.

While a program can have a combination of elements from all three approaches, it usually has a primary focus of one over the other (Spitzberg 1986, p. 5).

Gardner discourages the one-size-fits-all approach to leadership:

It is wrong to suppose that we can design a process that will start with a specific group of young potential leaders and

end with finished products. What we can do is offer prom-
ising young people opportunities and challenges favorable
to the flowering of whatever leadership gifts they may have
(1987, p. 3).

Advocates of leadership studies believe, in part, that the
malaise in the country can be partly blamed for the lack of
leaders driven by clear direction. Even Gardner laments that
in the late 17th century, when our population numbered 3
million, we produced six world-class leaders—Jefferson,
Adams, Washington, Franklin, Madison, and Hamilton. Where
are their equivalents today with a population of 248 million?
Are they among us but not tapped? (Gardner 1987, p. 24).

The leadership movement in higher education is premised
on both the availability of untapped individual leadership
potential *and* the belief that courses or programs can provide
the catalyst for the unleashing.

Despite obstacles of money, protection of disciplinary turf,
and cries of relativism, studies of leadership are very evident
in American higher education. Supporters believe that the
emerging leaders graduating from institutions of higher education must grapple with the civic crisis of modern society.
What is evident in all too many of the approaches, however,
is the emphasis on "individual" development rather than a
community approach.

Young potential leaders must be able to see how whole sys-
tems function and how interaction with neighboring systems
may be constructively managed. . . . If, despite all the dis-
couragements, a spark of enthusiasm for leadership is
ignited in any of our young people, our educational system
may well snuff it out. It does this in two ways. First, it places
enormous emphasis on individual performance and vir-
tually none on the young person's capacity to work with
the group. Second, the educational system—not necessarily
with conscious intent—persuades the young person that
what society needs are experts and professionals, not leaders
(Gardner 1990, pp. 159–60).

The pedagogy of leadership studies continues to be
debated. The notion that individual leadership is what is
needed, for example, may overlook civic leadership. Certainly

every sector needs persons who can guide organizations and ideas to fruition. For many reasons, however, not the least of which is that the national and global society is pluralistic and multidimensional, leadership development must be defined more broadly. It goes beyond the skills of one person to functions that people, families, communities, and even nations can exhibit. *Civic* leadership is about collective action, public will, and community (Morse 1989a).

The leadership theory needed for today may not be found in the traditional models like the "great man" or "great moment." The society of the 21st century needs leaders who understand diversity and choice and how citizens must act on their collective judgment if problems are to be solved. For these new leaders will not be asked to lead or direct in the traditional sense but must create a public space for people to come together in communities, in volunteer organizations, in corporations, and in all levels of government to discover their collective interests. To paraphrase William James's words, these new leaders must help find the "music within us" (Morse 1989a, pp. 441–42).

The corporate community has for many years viewed team-work as a critical dimension of solving problems and getting projects completed, and the notion is prominent in the literature on corporate leadership. *Leadership Is an Art* (DePree 1989) talks about leadership with words like "community," "commitment," "vision," "communication," "diversity," and "participation" and follows the work of Robert Greenleaf on the concept of servant-leaders—those who allow the followers to do their work. A Super Leader is defined as "one who leads others to lead themselves" (Manz and Sims 1989, p. xvi). This notion of getting people invested in solving their own problems is a recurring theme in every section.

This new dimension of leadership is not about one person but about communities of people and how they go about the business of doing their work. This theory of "group leadership" (developed in part by Ronald A. Heifetz and Riley Sinder [1988] at the Kennedy School of Government at Harvard University) argues that leadership not only creates action and direction on issues but in fact educates the public on how it does its work. The leadership trap it identifies is when the group (whether citizens or senators) *expect* the leader or leadership to solve problems. This dependency creates situations filled with disappointment and disillusionment. Even when leaders do find solutions, they may be thwarting the group's own capacity to solve problems.

The kinds of problems that citizens must grapple with are complex. The massiveness of poverty, homelessness, crime, drugs—all require a definition of the problem as well as possible solutions. The process of definition requires grappling not only with the facts but with values, tradeoffs, and choices. Who can do it effectively?

> *Only the group—the relevant community of interests—can do this work. It must do the sorting and learning necessary to define what constitutes a problem. It must make the adaptations and adjustments to the problem situation that most solutions require. Solutions in public policy generally consist of adjustments in the community's attitudes and actions. Who else but those with stakes in the situation can make the necessary adjustments?* (Heifetz and Sinder 1988, p. 188).

The leader moves from problem solver and visionary to teacher and facilitator. Success is more likely when the group works together as citizens toward acceptable solutions and recognizes the interrelationship of issues. As students are taught about leadership, they must understand the realities of public life or, for that matter, private pursuits:

- Difficult questions have no easy answers.
- A problem can be defined in many ways and thus have multiple possible solutions.
- Public action and movement require that the conversation be broad and diverse.
- Public policy solutions *require* choice among alternatives.

These lessons define our leadership crisis and imply that leadership theory requires a pedagogy to create a new way for making public decisions.

Creating the new reality of leadership for students as well as others is not an easy task. Thinking about different ways to lead takes four general directions:

> *1. It means going against their expectation that the leader can fix things for them—frustrating them in their initial desires.*

2. *It means holding steady as constituents, over time, begin to face their situation—maintaining one's poise, resolve, and capacity to listen when under attack.*

3. *It means helping constituents carve out of their messy situations discrete problems needing their attention and work—challenging assumptions regarding the situation and provoking the discovery of alternative problem definitions.*

4. *It necessitates managing the iterative process of devising solutions, making adjustments, and redefining problems as the situation changes and as constituents reorder their priorities along the way* (Heifetz and Sinder 1988, p. 190).

As leadership studies grow, this "civic" dimension is increasingly included. Leadership like citizenship is multi-dimensional. As many institutions develop a leadership component, they move beyond the narrow definition and get students (and themselves) to understand and practice a new brand of leadership that is inculcated in every aspect of life and work.

General and liberal arts education
One constituency believes that the real integrator for participation in common life should be the curriculum, and they find some supporters with the classicists. The liberal arts are seen as the equalizer, not the separator. Common learning allows students to see the connections of things, but interest in the composition of a general education curriculum to address civic skills seems to be lost (Boyer and Levine 1981). Those who argue that a general education curriculum is the institution's primary vehicle for teaching all students about public life assume that it will happen with special requirements. The topic of preparing students for the civic arts has sparked such interest that a volume of *Liberal Education,* "The Civic Purposes of Liberal Learning," was devoted to this theme.

The historical purposes of general education through three national revivals (1910–1930, 1943–1955, and 1971–1981) have shown a declining emphasis on civic education. Primary goals for the curriculum of the first two periods were educating for democracy and teaching citizens public responsibility; they were not for the latest period. While the evidence is not conclusive, it does indicate a waning interest in having the general education curriculum specifically address the development of civic skills. A description of the general education curriculum as more than a single set of courses emphasizes the need for clearly defined curricular goals that can be achieved in a variety of ways. While the purpose of the general education curriculum is crucial, the civics course is specifically discarded as a necessary part of general education (Boyer and Levine 1981, p. 51). Added to it is the continued debate about the role of disciplines in the general education curriculum. Boyer (1988) found that general education was the stepchild of undergraduate education.

> *Citizens may be born free; they are not born wise. There-fore, the business of liberal education in a democracy is to make a free man wise. Democracy declares that "the people shall judge." Liberal education must help the people to judge well* (Ward 1989, p. 29).

The goal was integrated learning that used the discussion method as much as or more than lectures. Students were active learners and if they were "good judges," they had mastered the art of critical questioning and thinking.

The assertion is widely held that a well-balanced general education curriculum by its construction will allow students to learn civic skills. Course sequences and disciplinary requirements are believed to give students the background necessary for a productive public life. Traditional liberal arts curricula have emphasized the rational development of the student at the expense of the emotional, however (Brubaker 1977).

> *Unless there can be a redress of the balance between reason and emotion, conventional liberal/general education is threatened with obsolescence and may even be terminally ill. The college should not be distinguished by its objectivity or neutrality but by its openness to "adversary" relations. It is the passions aroused by "confrontation" that give a sense of authenticity to what the student studies* (pp. 83–84).

A core curriculum must do four things to strengthen the role of an educated person in our society:

1. Help develop the student's capacity for self-analysis;
2. Educate about social goals, public purposes, and the ethics of citizenship;
3. Allow for practice with real-world problems and provide opportunities for leadership; and
4. Encourage students to have a personal sense of responsibility for the larger world (Cleveland 1981, p. 510).

Nearly a decade ago, writers called for new ways to educate for citizenship, urging colleges and universities to find ways to meet the urgent problems not through one course but through a whole range of learning in formal and informal education. While higher education cannot solve all the problems, it has a special obligation and can play a significant role. "Without any dilution of academic rigor, . . . civic understanding can be increased through courses ranging from literature and art to nuclear physics and industrial engineering" (Boyer and Hechinger 1981, p. 49).

The liberal arts/general education answer to civic preparation often includes the auxiliary discussion of values education, which affects the discussion of civic education in a clear way. Politics, as it is defined here, is about choice. The judgment needed to make those choices comes from value systems that are held as individual *and* collective. The literature on values education includes decision making, ethics, morality, and values and deals primarily with the institution's responsibility for the moral development of the individual student rather than the whole notion of developing collective or community values.[5] Rationalists from Cardinal Newman to Mortimer Adler believed that the liberal arts have no place for "values"; that is, human nature is rational and the rational life is one of "seeing, building, and contemplating" (Anderson, cited in Brubaker 1977, p. 71). These advocates in both American and European education believed that the academy's job is to inform student's minds, not their morality (Brubaker 1977, p. 75). Others disagreed, however. One of the primary failures of the liberal arts is its failure to define its role in values development.

---

5. See, particularly, Baum 1979; Callahan and Bok 1979; Fleishman and Payne 1979; Morrill 1980; and Warwick 1979.

The liberal arts college more than any other institution ought to provide the forum for enlightened discussion of those crucial matters, because the questions that are being asked about the character and quality of American life boil down to value *questions* (McGrath 1975, p. 11).

On receiving the Nobel Prize in 1976, Saul Bellow framed the quintessential challenge to educate for broader purposes:

When complications increase, the desire for essentials increases too. . . . Out of the struggle at the center has come an immense longing for a broader, more flexible, fuller, more coherent, more comprehensive account of what we human beings are, who we are, and what this life is for (Bok 1982, p. 69).

The very broad category of liberal arts and general education has the perspective that the substance of courses taught in certain ways and the knowledge of certain areas are the ingredients that prepare students for citizenship. The age-old topics of values, morality, virtue, and citizenship play a role in how liberal arts curricula are defined.

Civic or public leadership education
This approach to education for citizenship includes attention to different approaches to pedagogy and experiences. The development of citizenship should be based on the concept of a community of learners that can:

. . . trace itself from Aristotle to the current situation by having some "dynamic of interests" that help define the "good life." Helping students define their roles as citizens is the only way an understanding of the good life beyond private interests will emerge. Problems need to be confronted from the standpoint of everybody starting with his or her own perspective, but trying to understand a bit of a larger or public perspective (Ketcham 1987, p. 19).

The political or civic model addresses the question of what makes a good education for citizenship. The approach must be different and comprehensive; thus, "politics" is defined in a new, broader way:

*In a democracy, we need to be able to talk together. . . to
think together. Public thinking is not just analytical and logical; it requires us to explore together, to compare, to synthesize. If public politics requires such skills, surely the central task of a civic educator is to teach them. A student does
not have to be an adult to be a part of the public dialogue,
to learn to think with others, to learn how to make judgments about common purposes. . . . Not any experience,
but a direct experience in doing public work, seems to be
essential to learning public skills* (Mathews 1988, pp. 7–8).

Others define politics as the public life we share and the
choices we make on the norms and values of that shared existence (Arendt 1965; Palmer 1981; Pitkin 1981). Politics then
is not political science. It is the realm of all of life that requires
participation, civic skills, and the capacity to join with fellow
citizens, or "thinking as a 'we' in the name of public good"
(Barber 1984, p. 35). This notion of politics and its requisites
for citizenship requires "a different orientation from that
which is usual in academia. . . . Citizenship education is interdisciplinary because it focuses on a subject not on any one
academic field" (Minnich 1988, pp. 36–37). Usually placed
in the social science area, the revised "course" approach,
when treating the subject of civic education, is lacking. Con-
verting political science courses into civic education courses
entails five difficulties:

1. Course planning tends to be directed toward the discipline
   of the department where it is listed.
2. Courses reflect the interests and background of current
   faculty and their evaluation of what will "cover the field."
3. Covering the field is most often discipline driven. The
   model is not developing skills for the *praxis* of politics
   but skills relative to others in the field.
4. Course offerings lean toward preparation for further academic study, not larger societal roles.
5. While experiential courses provide opportunities for the
   praxis, they often do not have the academic credibility
   of traditional courses. Therefore, practice is not seen as
   education but training. The notion that practice is relevant
   to theory (i.e., politics to political science, writing to literature, painting and sculpture to art history) is often lost
   (Minnich 1988, p. 36).

Therefore, teaching civic skills is not a course or course component under one of the disciplines but is part of many courses and activities. "What we want is provision for experience informed by reflection, practice experienced within a reflective theoretical mode" (p. 40).

John Dewey supported Thomas Jefferson's belief that an educated citizenry was essential to a democratic society in his "progressive" transformation of the public schools. Neither education nor even participation is the answer for defining citizenship, however (Ketcham 1987). While participation is desirable, it is not the essence of preparation for leadership: "One can readily imagine poor government in a society where 'access' is easy and participation universal" (pp. 146–47). No, what we are striving for is not just more education, access, and participation—while all are good and necessary—but an education in republican citizenship that includes actual experience in governing, either through town meetings, school boards, or the "latter day equivalents of the assemblage of all citizens, giving them vital public space in which to learn and conduct their public business" (pp. 160–61). Jefferson believed that through experience, citizens who are more motivated toward the public life can make better decisions about elected officials and can expand the understanding of the notion of community and the higher order of good.

> *His ideal person, then, was self-reliant and self-actualizing, but this person was also profoundly, irreducibly political; he was both a creature of his* polis *and an indispensable participant in its ennoblement. The public and civic virtue required of the responsible citizen is, after all, a moral quality, a posture not quantifiable in terms of amount of time expended or amount of information accumulated* (Ketcham 1987, pp. 161–63).

These advocates of the radical approach to teaching civic education all speak to the importance of good examples. Parker Palmer challenged colleges and universities to think of themselves as a civic community, one that displays the virtues of good citizenship and provides for the entire community a space for the *praxis* of politics.

Palmer directed a Quaker living/learning community near Philadelphia called "Pendle Hill." Through this experience of living, learning, and deciding with a group of people day in and day out, "community" is defined in a new way:

Community is that place where the person you least want to live with always lives. Second year corollary: *When that person moves away, someone else arises immediately to take his or her place* (Palmer 1987, p. 20).

This somewhat facetious notion of community bears an important point as we think about teaching politics to college and university students and the skills that are needed for practice. Community means coexisting and at times growing, sharing, disagreeing, and deciding with people with whom you have no recognizable shared values. Politics is about finding that shared sense of life and putting it into decisions and actions. Higher education should think about this notion of community as a way to design the educational agenda. This sense of campus as community is integral to a new way of thinking about politics and how students, learning and living on campus, can facilitate it (Palmer 1987, pp. 21–22).

Civic education, like the liberal arts, is not about individual courses. A broader approach to learning that includes both content and pedagogy, it is as much about how we teach as what we teach. To argue over specific courses or theories or even pedagogies loses the point. Civic education is not separate and apart in the curriculum; it *is* the curriculum.

Other

These approaches provide only a framework for thinking about how civic education is best taught. Other initiatives contribute to this discussion. An emerging area is philanthropic studies. Researched and advocated by Robert Payton at the Center for the Study of Philanthropy at Indiana University and the Independent Sector in Washington, D.C., among others, philanthropy and volunteerism have become a significant theme in recent years. Courses on philanthropy in American life are offered at Babson College, University of Southern California, Tufts University, Baruch College, City University of New York, and others.

Courses in ethics and values have seen a resurgence in professional education. Harvard Business School requires incoming students to deal with difficult ethical dilemmas in a three-week minicourse. Columbia University's business school has required a course on social responsibility since the 1960s. Business schools join everyone from physicians to engineers in addressing the ethics of professional life. The Hastings Center in New York has done an extensive treatment over the years of the ethics required and challenged in professional life.

Finally, the emphasis on international education has contributed to understanding the larger world. Not designed as civic per se, the whole array of programs for study abroad, international studies curricula, and the increasing numbers of foreign students studying in the United States have helped broaden the perception of the world and its peoples.

Summary

The history of higher education reveals its civic purposes through time and how, given societal demands, it has approached fulfilling them. The different approaches to citizenship education frame the complex arguments over how students best learn skills and responsibilities in institutions of higher education today. The nexus of the discussions is that "the purpose of the educational system as a whole is to form and maintain the political community and to equip the citizen. . . with the means of going on learning all his life" (Hutchins 1974, p. 32).

Of course, many ways are possible to think about the political community, citizenship, and civic education: Individuals learn about politics, their own sense of responsibility, and their desired relationship with others through observing, talking, and doing in the public realm. Citizenship, as it is used here, implies participation. It is a process that is learned, relearned, and reinforced almost every day.

Even raising the issue of how people learn to do politics frames the larger debate about the nature of politics on the one hand and appropriate learning on the other. They will have to have their own day in court. For purposes here, the pedagogical discussion is directed at the kinds of skills needed for people living in the American polity. "First of all, we are all citizens and, second, we are all philosophers" (Adler, cited in Murchland 1988). What Adler is saying is that by virtue of our birth or naturalization, we share the rights and responsibilities of citizenship; by virtue of our humanness, we must decide what the role of the citizen in a democracy should be.

This notion of citizen-philosopher suggests that the common charge to all is that "we" must decide what the citizen's role should be and what will take us there. As Alice in Wonderland asked, "Which way ought I go from here?" Replied the Cheshire Cat, "That depends a great deal on where you want to get to. If you don't care, then it doesn't matter which way you go." The first step in civic education is deciding where you want to go in concert with others in the community, and it requires definition, pedagogy, and practice.

DEFINING THE SKILLS OF CITIZENSHIP

Understanding politics—how differences are resolved, authority defined, and shared interests determined—is a lifelong process. Throughout the course of life, individuals are politically socialized to act or think about their relationship to the higher social order, also thought of colloquially as "the system." This term has come to mean everything that is "out there" but particularly how things get done, who gets what, and who gets ahead. The concept of "the system" has helped define public life in a fractious, splintered way. The broader concept of the political or civic community described here is based on an equal, symbiotic relationship that unites citizens with "the system" and each other and begins to define the common life.

The role of citizens is one that acts in concert with others in collective ways. This transformation naturally requires an understanding of citizenship that is more vigorous and mutualistic than one that views citizens as private agents pursuing private interests in the political marketplace (Barber 1988, pp. 200–201). The notion of a different kind of citizenry raises the issue of needed skills. Thomas Jefferson's well-known assertion to inform the discretion of the citizens carried with it more, not less, democracy. The call for more democracy and the reframing of the citizen's role from the private "I" to the public "we" calls for a set of civic skills and values and a system that reinforces those concepts.

Learning new notions of politics, community, and citizenship requires different ways of thinking and acting. This process begins informally at birth. Formal civic education must come before students assume the responsibilities of citizenship, however:

> Some of it [civic education] should come after the student is old enough to reflect critically and creatively on the paradoxes and ambiguities that attend any discussion of the classical communal social ideals (Cadwallader 1983, p. 41).

Citizenship is not something learned automatically or evenly. Moral and civic attitudes are framed not only by observations and interactions but also by the environment in which people live. In doing research for *The Political Life of Children*, Robert Coles noted that he was faced squarely with the reality that we learn our notion of politics and our relationship to others from our parents, peers, teachers, the media, and our history. An interview with a young African-American woman showed these influences at work:

I learned my politics when I was a little girl. My daddy would tell me that I'm one hundred percent colored, and that means I'm one hundred percent ineligible to vote, and that means I'm supposed to be an American citizen, but I'm not one (Coles 1986, p. 9).

The imprints made on individuals early in their lives determine the lens with which the world is viewed. By the stage of adulthood, well-developed patterns and processes of thinking limit the acceptance of certain political alternatives:

Though existent political socialization does not determine the actions of each individual or commit the existing system to an unchanging perpetuation of the status quo, it should be clear that many types of loyalties, beliefs, and behaviors are made highly unlikely by early learning (Weissberg 1974, p. 174).

The assumption also exists, however, that schooling and higher education, in particular, can help galvanize certain civic skills with students during the critical college years.

Oscar Wilde's comment that "radical politics takes too many evenings" spoke to the timing and the requirements for active participation in civic life. The proposition that students develop their concept of politics and public life from osmosis, course sequences, acquired knowledge, or even by daily living is not enough. Becoming a responsible citizen takes time and deliberative efforts. It is important that the higher education community, in toto, think about how the next generation of citizen leaders will develop the civic skills necessary for a healthy public life (Morse 1988, pp. 1–2). This development can be encouraged in a variety of ways in a number of places. What higher education offers to the civic process is a setting, a curriculum, and a community all aimed at developing human beings for living in a public world.

The founding fathers recognized the tension in a system of varied interests. James Madison understood the limits that contending factions placed on each other in a republican form of government. While the inherent assumption of a cooperative, give-and-take approach to politics assumes a common interest among the factions, it does not promote the spirit of the common good. While the republican model is built on a shared community, it lacks the idea of a shared spirit.

> *Citizens need and would likely develop valuable negotiating skills—seeking out areas of agreement, focusing where and how to concede nonessentials. . . to protect more basic needs, displaying good humor to one's opponents, and all the other exceedingly useful means of working and living with people of fundamentally different views and interests* (Ketcham 1987, p. 149).

The primary civic task . . . is . . . to define the relationship with other citizens.

Real and valuable skills for operating in the public sphere miss both the understanding of and preparation for civic life if they do not address the last phrase, "useful means of working and living with people."

The primary civic task then is not to define personal relationships to "the system" or the political realm as such, but to define the relationship with other citizens. In the course of waiting in airports and shopping in malls, the diversity and complexity of that relationship become obvious. How often has it been pondered how the country can ever get anything done, given the broad range of interests, needs, and attitudes of 248 million citizens? The fact that it functions at all gives some support to the theory of representative democracy. But the question has a subliminal message about what *could* be done. If citizens had different ways to learn, think, and act civically, would that influence the way the nation as a whole thinks about its purposes? The hypothesis is yes, *perhaps.* "Our political behavior depends on our idea of what democracy is, can be, and should be" (Sartori 1987, p. 12), consistent with the thesis that the kind of society we have depends on the kind of people we are (Bellah et al. 1985).

Models of Political Life

Political behavior depends on the vision of a democratic society. If only one such vision existed, the task for determining the requirements and skills for citizenship would be very simple. Unfortunately, there are more than one. Citizenship has different requirements, given how the political system is perceived, and scholars have proposed different frameworks for understanding the kind of systems that exist, among them the difference between unitary and adversarial democracies

(Mansbridge 1980) and representative democracy (author-itative, juridical, pluralist) versus direct democracy (unitary and strong) (Barber 1984). Three general versions of democracy are used here as a working structure for thinking about politics that encompass versions of them: electoral competitive democracy, representative democracy, and participatory democracy (Weissberg 1974, pp. 174–82). While these three models are not all-inclusive, this framework helps to identify how people are socialized to act in one mode or the other. The view of politics has enormous implications for participation, pedagogy, and required civic skills.

In thinking about a new theory and practice of citizenship, one must recognize how citizens see politics. It is obvious that the political left and political right are rarely pure but go through dozens of permutations that depend on current issues, preconceptions, and the candidates themselves. To think of the political system as left or right, Democratic or Republican, is therefore not relevant in understanding how people see their place in the governance of society. To define the skills and pedagogy for citizenship, however, one must understand how the system can or could function. The three models provide a way to think about the citizen's role in society.

- The *electoral competitive democracy* model says that citizens have a right to choose their leaders. This model does not delineate basic freedoms and rights directly, but advocates claim that freedoms will exist if open competition is in place. (See Schumpeter 1950 for expansion of this concept.) It essentially represents special interest politics among the elected. Their interests (or those of their constituencies) are above public interests. This approach limits the rule of citizens in making decisions about policy.
- The *representative democracy* model goes beyond the electoral process in two ways: Leaders must be responsible to the electorate, and certain basic freedoms are spelled out and guaranteed. This form of democracy requires more of citizens and spawns involvement in interest groups, calls on citizens to express opinions on public policy issues, and stimulates other forms of nonelectoral political participation. Representative democracy requires that citizens be knowledgeable on issues so they can evaluate the performance of elected officials, support the electoral process, and be

able to judge public policy decision making. The primary criticism of this model is that it is oriented toward special interests, does not encompass the concept of a collective good, and fundamentally limits the citizen's role to participate once the vote is cast.

- The *participatory democracy* model is a different conception of politics from the other two. The nexus of this form is the belief that politics includes all private and public aspects of life, that citizens have control over their own lives, and that politics helps to develop individual personality and efficacy. Advocates believe that human potential is achieved only through direct participation. This model has been criticized as unworkable and unrealistic for modern technological societies, but the counterargument is that just *because of* the world we live in, politics is a part of every part of life and requires participation and certain competencies. This view of politics is seen as a foregone conclusion. A low level of competence among citizens is not an argument against participatory democracy but an argument to promote skills to support it (Weissberg 1974, pp. 179–82).

These three approaches to a democracy illustrate that the importance of certain capacities depends on the accepted view of the citizen's role in the democratic process. What then does each require? The first model, electoral competitive democracy, requires that the citizen be well schooled in the process of voting, actually do it, and have knowledge of candidates' abilities and platforms. This philosophy of politics narrows its perspective to government and the activities of elected officials. Involvement would exclude all other areas of life (schools, churches, corporations), even though decisions made in those arenas might affect the entire community. For this model to work, citizens must also exercise tolerance in letting different perspectives come before the electorate (Weissberg 1974, pp. 68, 176–77). According to a number of national surveys over the last 25 years, citizens who believe voting is their only option tend to be less personally efficacious (Pateman 1970, p. 58). Voting is the least significant act of citizenship: Citizens are defined by their membership in a community, not in their right to vote (Barber 1984, pp. 187–88).

Knowing the essentials of the electoral system (age requirements, registration procedure, location of polls and hours they are open, and accuracy and method of reporting results) is required in this model—as is the political will to vote, which may come with the belief in the system or through campaigns to educate citizens on the virtues of voting. The issue of tolerance is more than rote; it is a lifelong socialization process. It is also a part of the other two models. Defining tolerance or even advocating tolerance means different things to different people, and the skill is defined in terms of political talk: It is the skill to listen to and accept convergent points of view and opinions, not necessarily to change one's own but to provide for other perspectives. The criterion of tolerance also has within it the notion of political equality. Arendt agreed that for a democracy to work, citizens must be equal—in the sense that all have an equal voice.

The second model, representative democracy, includes voting, encompassing the vehicle for citizens' opinions on political decision making and guaranteeing basic freedoms. In addition to the skills and knowledge required of those who support electoral competitive democracy, advocates of representative democracy require skills that support representative government. This model includes the exercise of nonelectoral forms of participation through interest groups and lobbying efforts, among others, knowledge of public issues, the vehicles for monitoring the actions of officials and responding to those actions, and a background in the basic freedoms and the constitutional and legal guarantees available for individual protection (Weissberg 1974, pp. 178-79). This model shows a relationship of individual citizen to representative, representative to individual citizen, directly and indirectly. It focuses on individual, aggregated opinions and the responsibility of individuals to fulfill their responsibilities—I voted, I think, I want, I need, and so on. While it overstates the case, the clear message in the representative model is "you represent me" (an important distinction from the participatory model). An advocate of this model must have knowledge of the political system, knowledge of issues, and commitment to the electoral process.

Knowledge of the political system includes a clear understanding of how the political system works—the operation of the three branches of government certainly, but also the fourth branch (individual agencies, bureaucracies, interest groups, legislative procedures, congressional staffs, opinion polling, petitions, and the whole range of ways citizens can influence policy). More mundane are the ability to write letters and make phone calls to the right office, agency, or individual and the ability to find others with similar interests and concerns through interest groups, lobbyists, political action committees, labor unions, churches, and so on. Constitutional and legal knowledge refers to the citizen's ability to identify the basic freedoms to which all are guaranteed and to understand how those rights are protected legally. Finally, knowledge of issues comes from a variety of media, from print to audio to visual, and from conversations with others. Advocates of a representative system would support, but not necessarily value, dialogue between citizens.

Representative democracy can be learned through formal and informal systems. In the course of working with special interest groups or lobbying groups, the specifics of whom to contact when are usually available. Knowledge, particularly of constitutional freedoms, legal rights, and political systems, is probably best learned through the formal educational system, while information on interest groups and so on is available through libraries and targeted publications. Finally, representative democracy requires general knowledge of a society's inner workings. Such things as regulations for corporations, citizen assistance programs, and tax policies might all be in these citizens' repertoire. The relationship to other citizens is superseded in this model by the emphasis on making government work and leadership accountable. Advocates of this model would see the importance of citizens' interacting as watchdogs and would not see the role of citizenship defined by participation with others.

Supporters of the third model, participatory democracy, believe that private lives and public lives are intermeshed and that to engage in public work, a citizen must fully participate. The code of this model is that politics encompasses all of life.

> *Not limited to government—it occurs in the home, in school, on the job, and wherever else decisions are made affecting people's lives—democracy is realized when citizens effectively control their own lives* (Weissberg 1974, pp. 179–80).

The participants in this system are usually more self-actualized and personally efficacious than in the other two models. They believe that they can make a difference in every area of their lives. This method has traces of Athenian *polis* and the New England town meeting, with citizens taking a stronger role in public decision making (Pateman 1970, pp. 57–58).

The participatory model requires, first and foremost, and apart from the other two models, active participation. All citizens are expected to take part in some political involvement, whether it be through the electoral process or the local tax levy campaign or with a religious organization. Participatory citizens are willing to accept high levels of conflict and dissent to allow the process to achieve its best results. Tolerance and respect for individual views are apparent. These advocates need the capacity to analyze issues in terms other than cliches and political rhetoric. They do not want to depend solely on expert opinion; rather, they want to be able to understand and judge and make choices on public issues themselves. Finally, the participatory model is built on the interaction of citizens. Advocates believe that politics occurs among all people, not just elected representatives or bureaucrats, and that citizens are very capable of public participation. The minimum skills for the effective operation of citizenship in participatory democracy include political tolerance, voting, and knowledge of constitutional, legal, and governmental structures, which are also found in the other two. This model, however, requires skills to practice citizenship: political talk, thinking, political judgment, imagination, and the courage to act.

These participatory skills are often overlooked in society. They are most often considered highly personal and individualistic, not public and collective, and the skills are assumed. They do more than support participatory politics, however; they *are* participatory politics. A civic system that holds participation as its ultimate goal, however, deserves a warning:

> It is important to see that the civic tradition does not simply romanticize public participation. The dangers of misguided, fanatical, and irresponsible civic involvement have been well documented, and some of the most eloquent warnings of those dangers have come from the classical theorists of citizenship. The point, rather, is that the action of involved concern within an interdependent community provides the image for a collective enterprise in self-transformation (Sullivan 1982, p. 158).

This civic transformation requires that citizens act in concert with one another. People must move from the "I" to the "we." Further, for this discussion, they help to define the kinds of civic capacities that students should have. As the three models suggest, the skills required depend on the system desired.

Civic Skills for Public Participation

If civic life is defined beyond voting, what does it require? The three models of participation require different things from citizens. Knowledge is required in all three, but only the third, participatory democracy, emphasizes the critical ingredient of direct action. It is this element and its complementary skills that are missing in public life today. The skills for this new version of citizenship go well beyond knowing candidates' history or even knowledge at all.

> *Education for democratic citizenship involves human capacities relating to judgment, to choice, and above all to action. To be literate as a citizen requires more than knowledge and information; it includes the exercise of personal responsibility, active participation, and personal commitment to a set of values. Democratic literacy is a literacy of doing, not simply of knowing. Knowledge is a necessity but not a sufficient condition of democratic responsibility* (Morrill 1982, p. 365).

The skills for citizenship include the abilities to talk, think, judge, imagine, and act.

Political talk

The importance of political talk in the western political dialogue was first introduced when Aristotle identified *logos* as the divider between man and animal. The very center of an active democracy is talk. Talk is not just speech; it includes the whole range of communicative skills: listening, cognition, setting agendas, and mutual inquiry (Barber 1984, p. 173). "Political talk is not talk *about* the world; it is talk that makes and remakes the world" (p. 179). Talk is a way of creating and maintaining community, which requires "the use of the art of communication for the purpose of building bonds of affection and interest among those who comprise a public . . . " (Bitzer 1978, p. 80).

Talk is the linchpin in politics that allows citizens to define, create, dissent, confirm, and act. Its place in the political process is critical.

> *One finds it easy enough to see how talk might be confused with speech and speech reduced to the articulation of interests by appropriate signs. Yet talk as communication involves receiving as well as expressing, hearing as well as speaking, and empathizing as well as uttering. The liberal reduction of talk to speech has unfortunately inspired political institutions that foster the articulation of interests but that slight the difficult art of listening. . . . In a predominantly representative system, the speaking function is enhanced while the listening function is diminished* (Barber 1984, p. 174).

Talk is not unidimensional; it has nine distinct functions: the articulation of interests, bargaining, and exchange; persuasion; setting agendas; exploring mutuality; affiliation and affection; maintaining autonomy; witness and self-expression; reformulation and reconceptualization; and building a community as the creation of public interests, common goods, and active citizens (Barber 1984). The last, the creation of community, is the culmination of the other eight (pp. 178–98). Given the importance of talk, how do citizens learn about political talk? If each of the nine functions is examined separately, no pedagogy emerges. But taken in concert with one another, the direction is consistent.

> *I will suggest that a curriculum for civic education grows out of a series of "conversations" that should themselves exemplify the process of civic interaction we seek to instill in our students. The conversations themselves, then, model a different perspective on public talk than tends to be the norm. They start with the assumption that, while we all have opinions and can have pertinent facts, good talk does not consist of a trading of, or negotiating between, such preexistent stances and evidence. . . . At its best, the public is where we find—through conversation with others—a deeper level of understanding of our own opinions and a level of understanding of ourselves and others* (Minnich 1988, pp. 34–35).

The skill of public talk provides for citizens the ability to talk, listen, *and* act together for common purposes. It is the basic vehicle that allows people to work together and decide together. To learn the skill of political talk, citizens must *talk*. Public talk itself is a pedagogy. What citizens learn from talking with each other are new ways of relating and working with others. Pericles also had this notion of public talk when he said that the Athenians "taught themselves first through talk" before taking action (Mathews 1988, p. 97).

Thinking

The ability to think is not a singular activity, but a collective skill requiring mental interaction with others. The literature on critical thinking gives some insight into the concept. Critical thinking is a prerequisite for learning civic responsibility (Glaser 1985) that includes three primary elements: an attitude to thoughtfully consider problems and issues, knowledge of logical and reasoning inquiry, and the ability to apply those methods. The ability to reason dialectically broadens the mind beyond technical specialties and allows for different perspectives to be considered (Paul 1984, pp. 13–14). While critical thinking and the concept of political judgment are not synonymous, thinking is the vital component in the judging process. It is important for students to consider different views, comparisons, and contrasts in ideas as they read, write, speak, and listen, but the ability to do so is greatly lacking for most students and teachers must emphasize this ability in every subject area (Paul 1984). Although it is assumed that students are confronted with differences in opinion and thought in every area of their lives, dialectical thinking must be directly addressed. The skill is neither technical nor procedural, however; rather, it is principled and based on the individual's ability "to achieve command of a national language and our minds, and to use both as resources to make rational assessments of experience and human life. . . " (Paul 1984, p. 14).

The skill of critical thinking in a healthy democracy, in addition to helping individuals think about specific events in life in a more reasoned way, has the psychological dimension of making citizens feel connected to a larger world. The connection of critical thinking to an individual's civic life is one of the "necessary tools and skills [students need] to make sense of the social relations, material conditions, and cultural milieus in which they exist and their relationship to the wider society and dominant rationality" (Kretoric, cited in Brookfield 1987, pp. 53–54). At the heart of the relationship of critical thinking to the political life is its emphasis on asking the hard questions.

A readiness to ask why things are the way they are, a capacity to speculate imaginatively on alternative possibilities, an inbuilt skepticism of the pronouncements and actions of those who are judged to be in positions of political and economic power—these are fundamental ways in which the processes of critical thinking, analysis, and reflection in adults can be recognized (Brookfield 1987, p. 68).

Finally, Buber's metaphor of "the narrow ridge" explains another part of the judging process (Arnett 1986). The narrow ridge is "where I and thou meet," and it is at that point that community is formed. This metaphor suggests the move from the private to the public and the ability to discern different perspectives and points of view. "A narrow ridge perspective in communication and community considers both persons' concerns in a situation and the special roles played by each. . . . In dialogue, each individual must be willing to let the other's stance challenge his or her own, to test ideas while still affirming the personhood of the challenger" (Arnett 1986, pp. 73, 152). Political thinking, however, involves something other than critical, good, or rational thinking:

Public thinking is not just analytical and logical; it requires us to explore together, to compare, to synthesize . . . and to learn to think with others, to learn how to make judgments about common purposes (Mathews 1989, p. 49).

Political judgment

Talk and thinking are building blocks for another skill required of participatory democracies: political judgment. A longtime observer of the public policy process says that the American public responds in three ways to important public issues. First, they become aware of the problem, usually through the media, and their consciousness is raised about the seriousness of the dilemma. Examples are well known— public sentiments with the escalation of the Vietnam War, the revelations of Love Canal, and the more recent plight of the homeless. Second, after the initial shock of information, the public then begins to think through or work through what actions might be taken. Third, solutions are determined and a political compromise reached. The media are good at hyping the issue but do little to help the public complete the last two stages of the cycle (Yankelovich 1985). "To be excited about an issue but fail to think it through makes for the worst kind of citizen. A state of moral frenzy is not political judgment" (p. 9). Thus, we come to that often misunderstood skill—judgment—"the ability to bring principles to particulars without reducing these particulars to simple instances" (Minnich 1988, p. 33).

The concept of political judgment had its beginning in Ancient Greece. Aristotle talked of the ultimate human virtue, *phronesis,* which combined judgment and *praxis* (the good practice of the private man in the public realm). *Phronesis* becomes judgment that comes to action. "If I see what the situation requires but am unable to bring myself to act in a manner befitting my understanding, I possess judgment, but not *phronesis"* (Beiner 1983, p. 72). It is important, however, to differentiate between individual judgment and the civic skill or political judgment Yankelovich called for. Individual judgment is concerned with what "I" will do; political judgment is about what "we" will do. While the two share some characteristics, they perform very different functions in the political world. What then is "political judgment" and how is it exercised in civic relationships? First and foremost, it is about uncertainty; it is objective and subjective—and is required in sorting through the ambiguous gulf between opinion and certainty.

The wider recognition of the concept came through the writings of Immanuel Kant and a group of students and would-be students—Hannah Arendt, Hans Georg Godamer, Jurgen Habermas, and, more recently, Ronald Beiner and Benjamin Barber. All these scholars define and redefine the concept of judgment. Arendt particularly was responsible for the wider recognition of the term when she used the words "lack of reflective judgment" to describe Adolph Eichmann's evil origins in the Holocaust (1963). Arendt and other Kantian interpreters gave valuable insights into judgment as a cognitive skill. The "other school," led by Barber and other American pragmatists, sees judgment as a cognitive and a political activity (Barber 1988). For this discussion, this debate is not joined but focuses on both the cognitive and political functions of judgment and how they interact to affect civic life.[6]

---

6. For a complete discussion of the distinction of cognitive and political, see Arendt 1968, Barber 1988, Beiner 1983, and Kant 1951.

Despite its dimensions for the political, the capacity for judging is possible for all people. It gives citizens the ability to evaluate complex public policy issues and not rely on the declarations of experts.

> *The purpose of inquiring into the nature of judgment is to disclose a mental faculty by which we situate ourselves in the political world without relying upon explicit rules and methods and thus to open up a space of deliberation that is being closed ever more tightly in technocratic societies. . . . If the faculty is a general aptitude that is shared by all citizens, and if the exercise of this faculty is a sufficient qualification for active participation in political life, we have a basis for reclaiming the privilege of responsibility that has been prized from us on grounds of specialized competence* (Beiner 1983, pp. xi–xii).

Judgment has been thought of as something private, possessed only by individuals for their own use: "She has good judgment" is a sign of more cognitive detachment than of engagement in the political. Individuals cannot have political judgment alone, even in very personal matters, however (Barber 1988, p. 189). The process of judging requires that others are recognized and considered in the process of thought and action; exercising judgment is not a solo activity.

> *A common civic activity constitutes what we mean by political judgment. The journey from private opinion to political judgment does not follow a road from prejudice to true knowledge; it proceeds from solitude to sociability. . . . To travel this road, the private citizen must put her private views to a test. . . subject them to the civic scrutiny and public activity of the community to which she belongs* (Barber 1988, p. 199).

The kind of thinking that leads to judgment allows individuals to lessen the deference to rules and regulations and permits the judging of a particular situation from anticipated conversation with others: "We must have the capacity to accept the human condition of plurality. . . . Judgment (or taste) decides not only how the world will look, but who belongs together in it" (Arendt 1968, p. 223). Judgment then is the capacity to think with others about our collective lives and actions. It goes beyond individual needs toward consideration of common goals, requiring the ability to view particular situations from many perspectives. Kant asserts in *Critique of Judgment* that a need exists for a different way of thinking—we must "think in the place of everybody else"—calling it the "enlarged mentality" *(eine erweiterte Denkungsart)* (Arendt 1968, p. 220). Arendt calls it a prerequisite for judging and adapts Kant's view of it (Kateb 1983, p. 38).

Interest in judgment, especially public judgment and the ways in which that judgment can be exercised for the collective good, took on new dimensions after World War II. As the knowledge of the massacre of 6 million Jews became public, the horrified world questioned how the Holocaust could have happened. The war crimes trial of Adolph Eichmann, which Arendt reported and the world watched, exemplified in a clear, but shocking, way the outer limits of no public judgment. Eichmann followed the orders and planned the strategy that killed millions of Jews. He recognized no moral responsibility to judge on his own but simply to follow the rules and regulations set before him. Unfortunately, the rules handed to Eichmann were inhumane, immoral, and savage, yet he did not exercise thinking or judgment on that particular situation beyond orders he was given. At his trial, Eichmann admitted that he had been a part of one of the worst crimes against humanity in history, yet he said had he not followed the orders given him, his conscience would have bothered him (Arendt 1963).

It can be said that Adolph Eichmann lacked humane judgment not only because of his primary role in the deaths but also because of the manner in which he made his decisions. Eichmann acted out of personal ambition, thought of self, and exercised blind complicity. He lacked the capacity to think and thus to judge. Arendt called Eichmann thoughtless, contending that thinking is one of the conditions that causes people to abstain from evil. Arendt held "that a person's ability to say 'this is right' or 'this is wrong' in the world presupposes that he has stopped to think, felt the 'wind of thought!'" One of the by-products of thinking is judging; therefore, in some respects, thinking is the necessary requirement for judgment. Thoughtlessness is the absence of an internal dialogue. In Arendt's view, a thoughtless person who commits evil is different from a wicked person. To be wicked means overcoming the "thinking" partner, silencing all objections. Thoughtlessness means hearing no internal objections (Arendt, cited in Young-Bruehl 1982, pp. 279–80).

A democratic society is built on its ability to act collectively. Public judgment is required because politics is about the uncertainties that surround public issues. Because judgment implies that what we can know together as citizens we cannot know alone, it is imperative that educators emphasize and expose students to the value of diversity, pluralism, and the need to find common interests. But judgment is more than good, sound thinking. A helpful distinction between "judging insight and speculative thought" is that insight is based on common sense. "This 'good sense' discloses to us the nature of the world insofar as it is a common world. . . . Judging is one, if not the most important, activity in which this sharing-the-world-with-others comes to pass" (Arendt, cited in Denneny 1979, p. 264).

Imagination

The skills of thinking and judgment are joined by the ability to imagine. Judgment, in Arendt's view, is the ability to view the same problem from other's perspective through imagination. "While reason requires that I be together with myself in the conscious dialogue called thinking and the will requires that I be identical to myself, only judgment requires that I be together with my fellow man" (Denneny 1979, pp. 251–52). Thus, for the capacity for judgment to be learned, the use of the imagination is needed. Political imagination is the power to intend a state of affairs that does not yet exist, a way of inserting oneself into the existence through the future (Murchland 1988).

Judging therefore requires both thinking and the capacity to imagine a dialogue with others. Kant's treatment of imagination suggests that it is always in relation to others: Imagination, he said, is the condition of all thought. The Kantian concept contends that individuals must have the ability to view situations from the perspective of other people:

We do not judge as they might judge; our judgments are not identical with their judgments (which would be empathy), but we judge from their point of view. By the utterly mysterious power of imagination, that strange ability to make present what is absent and to make ourselves absent from our immediate perspective and present to some absent perspective, we are able to put ourselves in the other's position and see, not as he sees, but how it looks to us from his point of view (Denneny 1979, p. 264).

In a step farther, basic to public participation, citizens just imagine how they might change the world. "Judging . . . activates imagination by demanding that participants reexamine their values and interests in light of all the inescapable others—the public" (Barber 1984, pp. 136–37). Judgment, however, deals with particulars, while imagination is more commodious and deals with a broad range of general and particular considerations. Imagination makes judgment possible (Murchland 1988). Imagination is the condition of all thought that makes all other cognitive faculties possible (Kant 1951).

An exploration of how imagination should be a part of the college experience assumes that the primary goal of education is to develop the capacity of judgment so that students might imagine a different world (Smith 1987). What should be valued in higher education is not the right answer, but imagination. "Imagination is the power of the mind over the possibility of things" (Wallace Stevens, cited in Smith 1987, p. 20). Imagination has played a role in ancient and contemporary cultures (Kearney 1988), particularly in the perception of imagination from a mystical cosmic view to an individual internal and subjective capacity.

Courage to act

Beyond these four skills for a participatory democracy is the courage to act. Because of the uncertainty in the political realm, action based on judgment requires courage. It has been said that courage is *the* political virtue, because other skills become worthless without it (Denneny 1979).

Courage is best explained through example. The Danish citizens displayed exemplary courage during World War II. During the first part of the German occupation of Denmark, no attempts had been made to deport Jews to concentration camps as in other parts of Europe. In August 1943, however, tension had reached an all-time high in the country with the resignation of King Christian X and numerous acts of rebellion by the Danes. On September 28, 1943, an anti-Nazi, German embassy official, G.F. Duckwitz, secretly sent word that on October 1 and 2, the beginning of the Jewish holy days, the Jews would come under attack. Within 48 hours, more than

7,220 Jews had been contacted, hidden, and transported to safety by their non-Jewish fellow citizens. Only 464 Danish Jews were taken to the Theresienstadt concentration camp. This remarkable story illustrates both judgment on the part of the Danes *and* the courage to act on that judgment. The explanation is clear:

> *The courage of the rescuers did not come simply from their deep humanitarian commitment, from their sympathy for the persecuted, or from their hatred of the Germans. It was an idea of honor or pride shared by the entire people* (Goldberger 1987, pp. xiii–xv).

The courage to act was further confirmed in a new study of non-Jews who did or did not participate in the rescue of Jewish citizens. Using a sample of 682 individuals, the primary researchers looked for the sociopsychological factors that contributed to the courage to act on behalf of the Jews. The results show generally that rescuers were people who had a good relationship with their parents and extended family, had high levels of self-esteem from those relationships, generally thought that they could affect their circumstances, felt some responsibility for others, and tended to be more accepting of people different from themselves (Oliner and Oliner 1988, pp. 172–77). While growing up, they were taught, either directly or indirectly, to be submissive to authority. The rescuers were comfortable in thinking for themselves and did not tend to be awed by authority figures in any circumstance.

According to data, only 1 percent of the rescuers had parents who emphasized obedience versus 9 percent of the non-rescuers and 12 percent who did not refuse aid in a rescue but did nothing to prevent the situation (called "bystanders"). The Holocaust required public disobedience. The unquestioned obedience that was so apparent among the Germans is the hallmark of unequals; this kind of obedience (learned most likely in the home) was an end itself and facilitates adaptation to any type of authority—whether merited or demanded (Oliner and Oliner 1988, p. 162). This emphasis on obedience or submissive regard for authority can lead to the kind of blindness that prepared Germans for the success of the Nazis (Miller 1984). The rescuers showed concern for quality, personal attachment, and fairness. "The ethical values of care and inclusiveness that distinguished rescuers were not merely abstract or philosophical preferences. Rather, they reflected a key dimension of rescuers' personalities—the way they characteristically related to others and their sense of commitment to them" (Oliner and Oliner 1988, p. 17).

How people have the courage to act has everything to do with their view of the world (politics) and their role in it. The courage to act comes from the interaction of the other skills. In this nation, the civil rights movement was predicated on the civic capacity of a group of people to think, judge, imagine, and then act on a societal problem. While events and stimuli caused certain actions, the movement itself came from long years of practicing civic skills in hiding. The Southern Christian Leadership Conference's program on citizenship education and programs at the Highlander Center in Tennessee was instrumental in helping to develop those skills and taking them from private to public. Before the Civil Rights Act of 1965, most African-Americans could not participate in any of the political models described here. Their view of politics actually emerged out of, rather than evolved to, the representative model. Outstanding individuals like Dr. Martin Luther King, Jr., Rosa Parks, Fannie Lou Hammer, and Ralph Abernathy were critical, but the movement was a collective effort.

The courage to act can be costly. The resistance of Nelson Mandela and others to apartheid in South Africa meant decades behind bars. The years of labor unrest in Poland led by Lech Walesa put the world on notice that Communist policies did not work, but the leadership endured constant pressure from and surveillance by authorities. The prodemocracy movements in China and Eastern Europe have caused hundreds of deaths and imprisonments. All of these actions would cause citizens to ask whether taking action is worth it. Do things change? Certainly not every time or in every situation. But the Berlin Wall is coming down.

Summary

How individuals perceive democracy, the supporting political system, and the citizen's place and responsibility in it is the primary factor in determining the kind of civic competencies that individuals need. The individual political socialization process is affected by many factors, including the family environment, interactions at school and in organizations, and the picture painted by the media about politics and the public sphere. The three models of democracy discussed—electoral competitive, representative, and participatory—represent three very different views of the citizen's responsibilities in a democratic society, and each demands different skills. The three have overlapping functions and are not pure and distinct theories. They do, however, present different ways of thinking about citizenship that have strong implications for the way society works. The decline in voting over the last several decades, 20 percent since 1960 in presidential elections (People for the American Way 1988), for example, has focused much attention on "getting out the vote." The process of voting has almost superseded any discussion of other civic responsibilities and has caused quasi-acceptance of the electoral competitive as the predominant democratic model of democracy in the United States. Paradoxically, however, discussion is increasing on the importance of civic education in primary through secondary grades as well as in higher education. The implication is that while trying to encourage at least the minimum level of participation through voting, interest is strong in changing it as the preferred (at least in practice) political model. That being the case, a new way of thinking must be developed about the relationship of the citizen to the political. A movement is apparent toward a redefinition of what "commonwealth" means (Boyte 1989).

Five qualities are needed for democratic statecraft:

1. Observation—*the ability to observe with accuracy things as they are in themselves, "to know" whether the things depicted be actually present;*
2. Reflection—*which teaches "the value of actions, images, thoughts, and feelings and assists the sensibility in perceiving their connection with each other";*
3. Imagination—*the ability to modify, to create, and to associate;*
4. Invention;
5. Judgment—*to decide how, where, and to what degree . . . these faculties ought to be exerted* (William Wordsworth, cited in Schlesinger 1986, pp. 422–23).

These kinds of abilities needed for a democracy call for a new style of leadership and followership. "It require[s] leaders to be responsive both to constitutional standards and to popular needs. It require[s] followers to be informed and critical participants in the labor of governing themselves" (Schlesinger 1986, p. 429).

This recreating of our civic life requires skills beyond knowledge or subjective evaluations. It is more about attitude, personal efficacy, acceptance of new ideas, diversity, and opposing opinions. It is about using political talk, thinking, judgment, and imagination to create the capacity to act thoughtfully and prudently on critical public issues. By thinking through civic skills, we are beginning a conversation about the kind of political model that is more productive for America and how that might be attained. Higher education is an excellent vehicle for both identifying and developing civic skills. It becomes not a decision of "whether" we will be but "what" we will be in the political sense.

EDUCATING FOR PUBLIC LIFE

No one way is available to learn about politics and the citizen's role in the political, short of practice. But practice does not mean just doing anything; it means acting based on an understanding of how a democracy or a community should function. Living in concert with others is the essence of a democratic community, where, according to Barber, the connection between education and democracy begins.

The point where democracy and education intersect is the point we call community. For if democracy is a mode of associated living, then it is also true, Dewey has written, that "in the first place, the school must itself be a community life. . . !" (Barber 1989, p. 69).

Public life or community life denotes a larger participation and an interaction that is communal.

Public life or community life denotes a larger participation and an interaction that is communal. Where a student learns about citizenship then is not the issue as long as a pedagogy and environment exist for developing civic skills. Classrooms that generally provide theory can be just as strong for the practice of civic competencies. Civic learning can take place inside and outside the classroom, although vehicles must be designed to encourage and allow for it. Theory, practice, and reflection must be understood and initiated with other citizens to provide the framework for the civic life. The skills of talk, judgment, and imagination need a place to operate and create. We are reminded of Thomas Jefferson's cautions about allowing people to vote without reciprocal participation:

Jefferson had at least a foreboding of how dangerous it might be to allow a people a share in public power without providing them, at the same time, with more public space than the ballot box and more opportunity to make their voices heard . . . than election day (Arendt 1965, p. 256).

Colleges and universities can provide those opportunities by rethinking both the pedagogy and the experiences required to develop civic competencies. The responsibility does not lie solely with one department or discipline, the internship office, or elective courses. If civic education is to be comprehensive and real, it must be more than a curricular assumption and must encompass all disciplines.

The concept of civic education is partially one of freeing individuals to think beyond themselves in a broader social context. Therefore, the idea is not to fit students into existing molds or existing society. Civic education allows, as Jefferson suggested, that every generation think about its own governance and living.

> *Students should be educated to display civic courage. . . .*
> *This form of education is political, and its goal is a genuine*
> *democratic society, one that is responsive to the needs of*
> *all and not just of a few. . . . Critical pedagogy must draw*
> *upon the cultural capital that students bring to the class-*
> *room. . . . [They must have] the opportunity to speak with*
> *their own voices* (Giroux 1980, pp. 357–59).

No one way exists to learn to be a citizen. Even the Ancients disagreed over teaching methods. A translation of educational goals of today to the Ancient Greeks provides some interesting insight into the currency of the "what and how" arguments today (Stanton 1986). On teaching *arete,* the Greek term for wisdom and knowledge, they had trouble deciding on method. Plato said it could be learned only through living a reflective life. In his dialogue on education, *"Mero,"* he takes it farther and says that virtue is learned through philosophy, primarily the dialectic. The Sophists completely disagreed, saying that *arete* could be taught only through formal studies, memorization, and structured exercises. Isocrates held the middle view—that *arete* required reasoning, practice, and exercises. And finally, the Greeks believed, the political events of the time provided a context for learning. The real ideas and problems that emerged gave them some intellectual clay to mold. The following approaches are not the end-all or be-all, but they are a way to begin thinking.

Practicing Politics: Examples, Stories, and Experiential Education

The way to learn about the political is to engage in politics— participating in the common life and the decisions and choices integral to it. Learning how to participate, however, is a critical part of the equation. Students often have the desire to participate but not the skills or the vehicle.

Practicing politics and developing skills do not necessarily mean tangible activities. They can be simulated or experienced in other ways. Take, for example, the critical political skill, reflective judgment, that Immanuel Kant considered to be the antidote required to move from the private life *(sensus privatus)* to the public or common realm *(sensus communis)*. He saw judgment more like an art than a science. That is, he considered the task of judgment to be more like that of a weaver than a geometer. By using this metaphor of artisans, Kant gave some subtle instructions about teaching and practicing reflective judgment: Follow the rules of teaching and practicing art. When one thinks about how an artist learns, two ways come to mind: by observing and understanding the work of others (examples) and by practicing art with the guidance of a teacher or mentor (apprenticeship) (Tyson 1988, p. 11).

Examples can be taken from an unknown story or situation or from the student's own experiences. Examples are not distant cousins of the case study method; they retain the quality of good contextual stories rather than a rational, logical sequence of events. The situations exemplified provide a theoretical testing ground for students. "Theories can then be brought into discussion not as regnant, not as the answers, but to see if and how they illustrate (or obscure) the stories, the examples" (Minnich 1988, p. 41). The use of examples can broaden the classroom setting and allow students to practice public talk and public judgment using the concreteness of the example as their shared experience. Using stories to teach is another way to practice in the classroom. Hannah Arendt was a master of the aphoristic technique. She used images in stories to relate very complex ideas, but she used them as excuses for long narratives. "She did not tell the story of philosophy; she told the stories of the philosophers" (Young-Bruehl 1989, p. 1). The capacity to put feelings, customs, and experiences in a larger issue of reference allows people a distance that makes reflection possible.

Teaching political education almost *requires* consultation with examples. They are proxies for actually making judgments and are "as close as we can get to practice. They exemplify practice" (Tyson 1988, p. 12). The use of example, allegory, and parables has a strong history in literature and religion. From the Bible to Aesop's Fables to the Canterbury Tales, the influence of close observation on another's life and experiences has been used for everything from charity to greed. Practical politics is no exception. Using examples to teach politics allows students to reflect on their own views and understanding of democracy, but examples also have an inherent epistemology; that is, examples not only instruct through their substance but also through the imaginary dialogue that students can enter into with others (p. 12).

The apprenticeship pedagogy is a familiar component in higher education at the undergraduate, graduate, and professional levels. Internships, mentorships, and apprenticeships are widely practiced in the health profession, law, crafts, and trades. This kind of practice or training is needed by "art" if it is to be learned. Through the apprenticeship, an individual learns the nuances, short-hand verbiage, and insiders' understanding (Tyson 1988, p. 11).

The professions have well-established traditions for internships. Most people recognize the importance of medical, electrical, and legal apprentices. What is less clear is the logical practice for an English or math major. Or, even more abstract, what does a civic apprenticeship look like? (Hutchings and Wutzdorff 1988, p. 6).

The idea of a "citizen apprentice" is an attractive concept for civic education. It expands on the idea of practical application by emphasizing the roles of *doing* and *reflecting* over observing that all too often accompanies an internship or service-learning project. A discussion of ethical learning, using the metaphor of writing, emphasizes the importance of doing, particularly repetitive doing:

> *Learning morality is like learning to write. It is not like learning geography or mathematics. Learning how to write consists in learning a few elementary concepts . . . and then* doing *it . . . over and over and over, with the advice, recommendations, and corrections of those who already do it well* (Fullinwider 1988, p. 3).

Learning civic skills is benefited by practice, repetition, and experiences with others.

One example of a way that apprenticeships extend the civic component is found at the Center for Health Services at Vanderbilt University. The center, begun in 1968, created a coalition of Vanderbilt students, including undergraduates and law, medical, and divinity "apprentices," who provided comprehensive human care to communities in poverty-stricken east Tennessee (Coles and Davey 1976, pp. 14–16; Couto 1982). Not only did students "practice" their particular specialty; they also learned about the interrelationship of their work with others. This health experiment was really a civic experiment about cooperation, community, and dialogue. According to the director of the center:

We have three goals: to have students provide a specific service to a community group, to assist a community group in fashioning responses to a local problem or need, and to provide an important learning experience for students (Forum for Liberal Education 1985, p. 17).

The kinds of public learning where undergraduate students serve public policy internships can be required to make professional decisions on the job (Hofer, Sexton, and Yarnella 1976). These programs illustrate how the structure of the experience, not the activity, can be the civic experience.

The final category—experiential education—encompasses a wide range of activity. To make the connection with learning, according to Dewey, experiential learning must have two primary components—continuity and interaction. By continuity, he meant the application of prior experiences on new situations and issues; by interaction, he meant the interrelationship between the individual and the public world. These two factors together allow students to integrate prior learning with experience. Research has shown that this combination influences how decisions are made in groups or communities, while this process of decision making helps develop the judging capacity (Chiarelott 1979, p. 82). The notion that both past and future experiences influence the present decision is part of the process of imagining a dialogue with others that is critical to judging.

It follows that we cannot move forward experientially without remaining in continuity with what has been accomplished in the past. As Dewey himself asserts, present experience can expand into the future only as it is enlarged to take in the past (Pollock 1960, p. 179).

Experiential learning must be integrated into prior experience or to a theoretical or conceptual base to have educational basis. Said another way, the promise of this component is for students to reflect on both the general and particular nature of the experience. Curricula should include both action and reflection so that students can see the interconnection between what they do and the informing principles (Dewey 1954, p. 170).

A political science professor expresses his views on the importance of experiential education to his discipline:

> As scientists need their labs and artists their studios, so students of mankind need to use the "real world" as their laboratory. They must venture back and forth between classroom and the fields in which humanity labors so they can observe and explain the "scheme of things" (Muir 1983).

The protest movements in the sixties and seventies bore out this point. Students found that despite their knowledge of the "theory of social change," they did not understand how to put it into action in the political realm. Interest in the experiential dimension of politics grew from that discovery (Daley and Pernaul 1984, pp. 19–20).

The relationship of experiential education through disciplines and professions to public life is not quid pro quo, however; that is, experience in and of itself does not constitute applicable education. Just working in a lawyer's office does not validate the principles or theories of the American legal system. Rather, if experiential learning, service, or internships are to add to civic education, they must make up the components of other educational enterprises.

Other works suggest that theory and practice do not automatically connect (Argryis and Schon 1974; Kolb 1984). Kolb's notion is that learning occurs in a variety of modes and stages, that it is a dynamic process that continually integrates knowing and doing. Argryis and Schon contend that theory becomes integrated as students test their assumptions and hypotheses in the real world, creating a perceptual imbalance out of which emerges a way to act that incorporates both prior learning and current observations (Hutchings and Wutzdorff 1988, pp. 7–8).

The service-learning movement, popularized by cooperative learning programs at places like Antioch College (Ohio) and Berea College (Kentucky), shows that theory and practice are interconnected and enhanced by each other. The notions of personal growth, exposure to different ideas and cultures, and application of classroom learning to real-life situations enhance and reinforce learning. The approaches run the gamut from year-long internships in Washington, D.C., to the 4-1-4 interim calendar that allows one month each year for experiential education (Gordon 1976, pp. 112–13). Service-learning, like classroom learning, includes many different approaches and criteria. For example, the Phillips Brooks House Association at Harvard, the community service organization, requires students to originate their own projects and then write detailed proposals to fund them (Toufexis 1987). Service-learning advocates believe that the experiential should not be separated in the curriculum. The National Society for Internships and Experiential Education in Raleigh, North Carolina, has researched this area extensively (1988, 1990).

The combination of service and learning seems so important—for it demonstrates clearly that intellectual challenges and the exercise of concern need not be regarded as rivals, each striving for time in an already overcrowded syllabus (Dickson 1982, p. 42).

Using apprenticeships, examples, and experiential education to "practice" politics requires more than the singular activity. These pedagogies must share certain characteristics if they are to contribute to a student's learning. Four criteria should be considered:

- *Concreteness.* Learning must be based on the student's experiences.
- *Involvement.* The student's wide-ranging feelings, emotions, and interests must be connected.
- *Dissonance.* Learners must briefly be thrown out of balance to move them toward greater understanding.
- *Reflection.* One must be distanced from the actual experience to see meanings and interconnections (Hutchings and Wutzdorff 1988, p. 7).

These requirements imply that if practice is in fact to be effective, it must be closely linked to a broader range of learning and experience. If not, the experience itself will not automatically provide the student with a relevant educational opportunity.

Using Specific Knowledge to Learn about Politics: Classics and Classroom
While reflective experiences bridge the world of the "practice" of politics and the theory of politics, one can learn about the

civic life in the classroom. This topic gets almost strangled by the debate over the curriculum. The debate is about the kind of knowledge needed for a good civic or political education. The most traditional is the study of the ancient forms of democracy and republicanism, and the Great Books and minds that supported them. It includes the formation and decline of ancient culture and the truths that emerged from those events. Advocates believe that a political education without the Great Books is in danger of cultural relativism and gives students no absolutes on which to judge right, wrong, or their own opinions. Although the study of the Great Books as the formation of the curriculum is not widely used (exceptions are St. John's in Annapolis and Santa Fe and some special programs within traditional liberal arts programs), it has received vocal support from people like Allen Bloom at Chicago and former Education Secretary William Bennett, both ideological descendants of Leo Strauss. Most institutions struggle for the happy medium.

The debate about the Great Books, however, is joined by those who call for some commonness in learning among students. When asked which books young people should read, the philosopher George Santayana replied, "It doesn't matter as long as they read the same ones" (Atlas 1988, p. 24). This argument, called the "canon controversy," was heard loud and clear when Stanford University decided to change texts for courses in western civilization. Cries of cultural relativism and accusations of administrative ignorance, irrationality, and intimidation were heard. This controversy has, at its core, the assumption that if the right books, theories, or courses are not taught (or vice versa), then students are irrevocably doomed to a life of uncivil mediocrity. These advocates believe that a base of knowledge is required for participation in the polity and that that base most likely rests with the classical thinkers. The opponents charge that those Great Books are fraught with sexism, racism, and ethnocentrism and do not reflect modern values.

The point must not be lost that the classroom can provide more than just theory impacted by the lecture method. It is in fact a "public space" where community can be practiced. The relations between students and the faculty member, students and other students, and faculty to other faculty reflect the recognized and respected values. An authoritarian environment obviously is not it. What can be built is a cooperative relationship between equals (not equals in terms of knowledge perhaps, but equals in the sense that they have the right to be there and to participate). Classrooms can be a version of Edmund Burke's "platoons of democracy."

Politics can actually be simulated in and out of the classroom through a series of well-defined situations that allow students to "practice" the civic skills of listening, public talk, judgment, and so on. A number of exercises have been developed. One is a board game developed by the Roosevelt Center in Washington, D.C. Called "Debtbusters," the exercise gives the players a chance to "solve" the national debt crisis. Another is the issues series developed by the nonpartisan National Issues Forum used on some campuses. Based on the concept of the town meeting, the exercise allows students to grapple with public policy issues from various perspectives. Some topics available include AIDS, crime, freedom of speech, and the environmental crisis. The purpose of these exercises is not to provide more information but to help students find their shared concerns (Mathews 1982, p. 273). Allowing students to "work through" the complexities of issues like debt or drugs can be important learning devices.

Students (and all of us) need opportunities to express themselves, listen to others, and weigh opposing positions. Extensive research on younger students shows that in cases where teachers encouraged the expression of opinion in class, students showed more tolerance of different views and a greater willingness to listen to the ideas of others. Students' being allowed to express their opinions and see that they were respected was a positive predictor of greater knowledge of citizenship. Positive educational experience occurs when the climate and the content of citizenship are congruent. An extensive literature review concludes that the most important contribution a teacher can make to enhance and develop democratic skills and values is to allow students to freely express their opinions in the classroom, contending that to do so is more important than the inclusion of any particular subject in the curriculum (Ehman 1980, pp. 98–119).

The idea of free expression in a classroom setting is not natural for some teachers, and a program has been developed to improve teachers' ability to reflect on their classroom processes (Elliott 1980). Called "classroom action," it encourages discussion in class before calling for premature consensus and emphasizes the importance of hearing all opinions, not just one (the teacher's). This process allows the teacher to simulate and reflect on actual classroom situations and be conscious of the dynamics that may inhibit the free flow of ideas (pp. 308–24).

Many advocate civic education's including certain basic facts irrelevant of the pedagogy, classroom environment, or relationship of teacher to students, believing that a course in "civics" will be adequate preparation for citizenship. They believe that teaching traditional American treatises of Madison, Jefferson, and Hamilton and the basic documents like the Constitution and the Declaration of Independence provides the foundation of citizenship. This approach to civic education emphasizes the facts of American democracy, its history and structure, and the role of government with citizens as fundamental checks and balances on the electoral process. This group might also include political theorists who believe that understanding the comparisons of liberalism to republicanism to socialism to communism will allow students to judge their own system of government. They equate knowledge of the governmental and political system with the ability to manipulate interests with the system.

They join another group of educators called the "number crunchers" in the "factual" approach. These individuals look at politics through trend lines, sociological changes, and public opinion polls. Attitude surveys, political perceptions, and voting patterns allow them to create a picture of politics driven by shading on a topographical map. They predict politics and teach that politics is influenced by forces like the economy, race, and special interests that cause the political landscape to shift, not by the political will of citizens. While these descriptions are extreme, they are intended to depict the generic approaches to citizenship and how they can manifest themselves in teaching.

All too often, however, teaching the civic skill is left for political scientists or professors of government. While that discipline can and does contribute to civic education, so can many others, given the structure and content of the course. In the scientific field, for example, civic education is enhanced by the same values and attitudes that encourage scientific inquiry (Hickman 1982), and contributions to political education are made through process and content. Biology students, for example, can learn about citizenship. First, students should know about public policy questions where individuals as well as society are in conflict. Then they should learn to analyze the problems and their solutions using a political and social framework (Oliver and Shaver 1966). Science provides a useful "laboratory" for learning about citizenship:

> [Both] share the common premise of truth as a commodity uncovered and constructed, not revealed. If matters of public policy emanated from some source that all could accept as infallible and all-seeing, citizenship and the education that supports it would be both meaningless and irrelevant (Hickman 1982, pp. 359–60).

A values approach in an introductory anthropology class helped students develop an intellectual and judging process to operate in a political world where no absolutes exist but contradictory viewpoints and difficult choices abound (Robbins and DeVita 1985, pp. 252–53). This approach allows the teacher to shed the role of expert and become an active learner with students as all wrestle with tough problems.

Despite the orientation of one emphasis of knowledge over others—or classroom over experiential—all pedagogical approaches are meaningless to the enhancement of political life unless an impetus exists to use these skills.

> Citizens are not saints: They need not become oblivious to the sacrifices involved. They must develop an orientation toward public life that causes them to incorporate a feeling for the good of the whole into a sense of what is good for oneself. One's own identity comes to represent a merger of private and public (Landy and McWilliams 1985, p. 54).

This commitment to the common or the higher order can come through knowledge or practice, but it is most likely to be connected with actually being in a community.

The role of the classroom, faculty, and teachers is critical to how students perceive themselves in the larger world. Despite the influences of family, media, peers, and acquaintances, the classroom setting provides an excellent opportunity to mirror positive political skills.

> [The faculty's role] would have a salutary effect on society as a whole if every college teacher of a course not attended primarily by majors in his own discipline would ask himself

at the beginning of each academic year what contribution his instruction will make to the effectiveness of the private and the public lives of his students. And in this exercise of self-appraisal, he could well keep in mind Montaigne's admonition that the purpose of education is not to make a scholar, but a man (McGrath 1975, p. 15).

Learning Politics through Community

"Community" has different meanings for different groups. In this context, it means that living, organic environment where faculty, students, administrators, and townspeople live, work, and act together. In the ideal, it is a community of learners bonded together by common goals.

Designated activities and circumstances make a higher education community different from other forms of communities, however.

The university is a community devoted to the preservation and advancement of knowledge, to the pursuit of the truth, and to the development and enjoyment of man's intellectual powers. Furthermore, it is devoted to the pursuit of these goals collectively, not merely individually. The public discourse is not a mere means to the private activity of research, as John Stuart Mills seems to have thought. Rather, that discourse is itself one of the chief goods to be found in a flourishing university. It is precisely this devotion to an essentially collective activity that makes the university a community rather than an aggregation of individuals (Wolff 1970, p. 128).

This notion of campus as community is illuminated by Dewey's differentiation between a local community and the Great Community. He used local and Great to mean local or state versus federal. The local community provides a nurturing, relational quality that can never be found in the larger community. The day-to-day, eye-to-eye interaction in a small community has no substitute. The proximity of community members and the ability to deal with problems and issues directly give us the kinds of skills that will allow us to interact with strangers.

Democracy must begin at home, and its home is the neighboring community. . . . Whatever the future may have in

*store, one thing is certain. Unless local communal life can
be restored, the public cannot adequately resolve its most
urgent problem: to find and identify itself* (Dewey 1954,
pp. 213, 216).

It is this practice of community that is needed.

One way to encourage community is a campuswide conversation with activists, politicians, and academics and students to address the question of what makes effective citizens
(Minnich 1982, pp. 37–39). The conversation would be joined
to one with political thinkers and those wise about public
life. These conversations would then be shared with those
on campus who have taught courses or led programs aimed
at civic education with the notion of deciding together what
needs to be taught and how. The kind of community exercise
would be a civic experiment in itself and could produce a
new way of reflecting and thus teaching new approaches to
political education.

Another approach is to think about community within the
academy as a way to strengthen the educational mission of
the institution. The alleged collapse of civic virtue in all of
society, the opinion that higher education should respond
to this civic crisis, and the need for higher education to offer
more interdisciplinary and value-oriented work suggest that
the answer lies beyond cosmetic repairs and requires reacting
for the "underlying nature of our knowledge itself" (Palmer
1987, p. 22). "The *way* we know has powerful implications
for the *way* we live" (p. 25). Perhaps a radical change in epistemology and pedagogy is necessary. The most common, integrated strategies in teaching and learning will fail if the basic
philosophy does not change:

> *You cannot derive communal ways of teaching and learn-
> ing from an essential anticommunal mode of knowing.
> The pedagogy falls apart if the epistemology isn't there to
> support and sustain it* (Palmer 1987, p. 25).

Residential life provides an excellent setting for consciously
learning about community and how it can operate, as do
extracurricular activities. Students active in student government, however, often are left with a narrow view of win-lose
politics. The interests of the larger community and their relationship to it are often left sadly lacking.

Education in citizenship must be a living component for students every day and be mirrored in every aspect of campus life.

Learning democracy was not accomplished through sterile civics or citizenship courses. It could not be done just by reading the Constitution or writing essays on the different functions of the legislative, executive, and judicial branches of government. Democracy was a lived *process, and it invariably involved adults' attempts to change some aspect of their personal, occupational, and social worlds* (Brookfield 1987, p. 174).

Great examples of this kind of learning are the Highlander Folk School and the Danish folk schools it was patterned after. Founded in the 1930s by Miles Horton, the Highlander is located in New Market, Tennessee, and has, for the last 50 years, been instrumental in training many community organizers and activists. The center has been at the nexus of the southern labor union movement and involved in civil rights and more recently miners' rights. Highlander helped "students" develop the capacity for individual and group problem solving using very real injustices. It was not politics in the abstract but issues that affected day-to-day living that people could connect and identify with (Adams 1972). Horton understood from his observations of the Danish folk schools that people had to have a place to learn the skills of participation and action.

Horton knew that he must get behind the common judgments of the poor, help them learn to act and speak for themselves, help them gain control over their daily lives (Joseph Hart, cited in Adams 1972, p. 110).

These lessons show the importance of community and politics in context. Students, like all people, learn from the community in which they live, be it a family, a dormitory, or an apartment. The challenge is to structure the college environment like a community with shared interests. The separation between faculty and administration, or between disciplines, sends clear signals about the campus's idea of politics and community.

The key to studies in citizenship is to allow students to perform the "natural" acts of civic participation in an academic or community setting. This process could include different disciplines and approaches but should draw on three general components implied in the research:

- A theoretical or cognitive component that informs students in the democratic tradition and illustrates the responsibilities and requirements of public life;
- A reflective component that allows students to consider real issues and the choices surrounding their solutions; and
- The experiential, which allows students to "practice" public leadership in a local setting.

Civic education can be accomplished only through a marriage of knowledge and practice. "Not only must academic learning be complemented by action, but active learning must be connected to an exploration of the concepts and traditions that underlie democracy" (Schultz 1987, p. 17).

Conclusion
The concept of citizenship and its pedagogy will remain abstract concepts if they are not debated and discussed with the same vigor as other educational goals. As part of a national project funded by the Exxon Foundation and administered by the Kettering Foundation, representatives from colleges and universities were asked to answer the following questions based on their own experiences. Though not definitive, their responses provide some guidance on ways that higher education can teach a new model of leadership (Morse 1989b, pp. 3-4).

How do people learn about citizenship and politics?
- Civic preparation occurs when you move beyond familiar circumstances, outside the curriculum, outside the neighborhood, or outside personal values to explore new perspectives, attitudes, and beliefs.
- Civic education is aided by being able to make connections, seeing causal situations and outcomes, and understanding the relationship between the individual and the larger community.
- A sense of our political selves is developed when we see something wrong and join with others to find remedies.

We are politically empowered when we can talk with our neighbors about an issue and act on that talk.

- How you feel about yourself politically is correlated to how you learn or are taught about politics. We mirror our parents and peers; the sense of our ability to affect or participate depends not only on what has been observed but also on how individuals are treated in any given situation—at home, in the classroom, or in daily interactions.
- A civic interest is often driven by the special or "hot" interest at hand; these issues deflect attention from a larger view of public responsibility and public policy. Specialization of knowledge and special interests challenge our concept of generic citizenship.
- Civic education includes being able to recognize the interrelationship of issues and look for the implications of the larger system. Our interest in issues can be either public or private or both simultaneously. Understanding the private aspect of issues helps determine where the public agenda might focus.
- Civic participation is difficult to learn from nonpractitioners.

What are civic competencies?

- Understanding the fundamental processes needed to maintain the appropriate interaction between government and its citizens.
- The ability of individuals and groups to talk, listen, judge, and act on issues of common concern.
- The capacity to imagine situations or problems from all perspectives and to appreciate all aspects of diversity.

How can campuses promote civic skills?

- Develop a living and learning environment that is an example of a working civic community.
- Encourage students to be active, educated participants in the definition, discussion, and solution of community problems in and out of the classroom and emphasize the importance of talk, discussion, consensus, and different points of view.
- Integrate the importance of civic responsibility into the process of student development; allow the student's self-image to expand from introspection to extroversion.
- Teach politics (or any subject) in new ways; push beyond the traditional view and allow for the development of new

skills; establish ongoing conversations (creating a space) on campus or in classrooms for students to practice civic skills; foster a community where individuals are called on to act and respond to issues in a different way. Be an example for students.

• Have a campus or community scheme that brings various players together on a regular basis as an opportunity for individuals to recognize, appreciate, and manage the diversity that exists in any culture or community.

Education for public life cannot be assigned or segregated. It occurs almost everyday no matter where we are. It may not be direct or overt, but some subliminal message comes along to reinforce or challenge a previously held belief. Colleges and universities have a great opportunity to prepare students for citizenship in new ways and in new environments. The key is that everything on campus has a political replication and the community is responsible for the vision it constructs.

The methodologies listed earlier all have a part in teaching undergraduates. Circumstances may determine where primary emphasis should be, but neither is the predominant vehicle. Colleges and university communities must decide for themselves and determine the appropriate balance.

Teaching politics has and will take on different forms and approaches. To avoid the topic because of its lack of pedagogy, however, reverts the conversation to the assumption that taking the right courses in the right sequence will make a student civically prepared. It is time to think clearly, consciously, and collectively about what citizenship is, how it is developed, and where it is placed in the institutional mission.

Perhaps it is time to stop complaining about the needs of society and worrying about the fate of the canon and despairing over the inadequacies of the students, which after all only mirror our own. Perhaps the time is finally here to start thinking about what it means to say that community is the beginning and end of education: its indispensable condition, its ultimate objective. And time then, if we truly believe this, to do something about it in words and in deeds (Barber 1989, p. 72).

RENEWING PUBLIC LIFE THROUGH ACADEMIA: Implications

Higher education has in recent years introduced a plethora of techniques to engage students for higher purposes. Most colleges and universities are grappling with how general education, community and public service, studies of leadership, and a whole range of other ideas fit with their educational goals. Somehow, within all these efforts are common threads, but rarely are the connections made. The common thread is simple—getting students to think and act beyond themselves. Each thrust does just that. General education broadens students' exposure to ideas and disciplines. Community and public service allows a student to both serve and connect theory with practice. Leadership education clarifies ways that problems can be solved collectively. The critical issue for higher education is to make these connections through the curriculum.

College: The Undergraduate Experience in America tracks through undergraduate education from all vantage points, looking at mission statements, academic programs, and student life. The recurring theme of the book, however, is how the undergraduate experience helps students place their lives in a larger context. This notion of public-spiritedness is what civic education is all about. The book goes so far as to recommend that every student complete a service project either in the community or campus as part of his undergraduate experience (Boyer 1988, p. 218).

The suggestion is a good one, no doubt, but solves only part of the problem. Service as an educational goal must pervade all areas of the institution. But neither service nor any other single approach is adequate. If a college or university is serious about preparing students for responsible citizenship, then that goal must be institutionalized, not set apart. It requires that the institution do four key things:

1. Have a campuswide conversation and deliberation about what citizenship means and the preparation needed.
2. Understand the realities of what is currently happening on campus (either in the classroom or extracurricular) to support that preparation.
3. Ask students and faculty in each discipline or major to think consciously about how that curriculum can or should prepare students for responsible citizenship and how it relates to the whole.
4. View education for citizenship as a recognizable, measurable, and assessable educational goal.

Higher education cannot be expected to perform a civic miracle with every student. Other factors have made strong imprints on individuals long before college. But institutions can have some say about the kind of environment where a student lives for a period of years. It can create a community that works. It can provide situations for students to sort out their own feelings about civic responsibility. It can challenge new ways of thinking about problems and their solutions, about differences, and about possibilities—what Barber talked about when he referred to a strong democratic community, a community of citizens, not individuals, who are empowered to act. A strong democratic community, however, transforms people but it does not subsume them.

> *Their authority is preserved because their vision of their own freedom and interest has been enlarged to include others; and their obedience to the common force is rendered legitimate because their enlarged vision enables them to perceive in the common force the working of their own wills* (Barber 1984, p. 232).

The struggle of colleges, said Boyer, is to maintain a balance between individual and community, which is, of course, *the* civic challenge. Colleges and universities have lost their conception of community. When the walls came down and the gates were left open, education experienced an identity crisis. Is the primary task to contribute to the betterment of society or to the betterment of individuals? The answer, of course, is "both."

We know that the ability to participate in politics has much to do with how an individual envisions the public realm and himself as a citizen in it. That vision of the larger civic life comes from years of political socialization before the student ever darkens the door of a college or university. Statistics about parental influences, income levels, and media communications confirm that people's attitudes are made up of what they hear, see, experience, or read. A study of school children showed that middle-class students tended to be more personally and politically efficacious (Greenstein 1965). They believed they could change things. When asked whose advice they would seek when voting, middle-class children said their own, lower-class children the teacher.

These revelations are not new: Issues of authority and power are learned early. What does it say about teaching the skills and responsibilities of citizenship in higher education? It frames the problem thus. Students come to college with a well-established sense of reality. The job of higher education is to create an environment that supports students' positive feelings about their own efficacy and also gives them the political skills to participate effectively and act courageously. "The task of education is to prepare students for the task of renewing a common world" (Arendt 1968, p. 196).

The Civic Conversation

At the 1989 meeting of the National Society for Internships and Experiential Education in Santa Fe, New Mexico, one panelist asked participants to write a 25-word want ad for a citizen. Although it sounds easy, it was not. People struggled with what kind of person that might be, and their responses ran the gamut. Some wanted citizens to be skilled in communication, others wanted people with imagination and insight, and still others wanted technical skills. The exercise, however, caused people to grapple with what citizenship means and how one is prepared for it.

This monograph is intended to be a requisite for a civic conversation. That is, students need some grounding in citizenship and what that term means as a guiding principle for their development and attitudes. The lessons from the Athenians and the early Americans like Jefferson and Madison provide reference points for thinking about citizenship today, not models to be replicated directly. The inherent inequalities and the social system on which they were based are very different from today's. They are good starting points, however, and have some lessons to teach.

Literature reviews tend to be collections and analyses of research done by others in a variety of ways. They provide background on a topic, pegs on which to hang other research, and primary research complete with data and analyses. This monograph has tried to define another purpose: to create in the reader's mind a dialogue on the topic. Like friendship, the term "citizenship" causes a mental reflex that brings the abstraction to reality. An individual's ability to understand friendship or citizenship has to do with his or her own experiences or his or her observations of others. Reading about it in a book or even having the concept described analytically does not have the same effect as articulating a personal vision of it or experiencing it. The purpose here is to do just that:

The task of education is to prepare students for the task of renewing a common world.

to present facts, analyses, and ideas about citizenship or political education as the basis of a larger dialogue on campuses.

Many of the writers and thinkers mentioned in the monograph are part of a national conversation about this notion of civic education and the vision of the political world. People like Benjamin Barber, Frank Newman, Elizabeth Minnich, Freeman Butts, Ernest Boyer, Robert Payton, David Mathews, Ruel Tyson, Susan Stroud, Donald Kennedy, John Gardner, Jane Kendall, and Ralph Ketcham are in conversation with colleagues and others to try to define public life. We should all be in such a conversation in our communities.

Organizing an institutional conversation will not be easy. It will require time for groups of faculty, students, and administrators to think and rethink their definitions together. A framework for organizing should include several parts:

1. *A statement of purpose.* The entire campus community needs a clear understanding of the issue being addressed to help eliminate the inevitable conversation stoppers. The task is to define what a responsible citizen should be able to do and how the entire undergraduate experience develops those abilities. The conversation is not about restructuring general education, debating the merits of community service, increasing the student affairs or housing staff, accusing colleagues of not doing their part, instilling political partisanship, threatening the viability of the liberal arts, or trying to limit the power of the faculty. It is about responsible citizenship and the academy's role in it.

2. *Participants in the conversation.* For the dialogue to have the most impact, students, faculty, administrators, and townspeople should participate. It is the kind of issue that should not be delegated to an ad hoc committee. It will be a rigorous debate and everyone should have his fair share of air time.

3. *Organization and reporting.* The first round of conversations should be interdisciplinary. The advantage is that so much of campus life is narrowly defined by disciplines and specialties that it would give the diverse community an opportunity to think together. The groups should be small enough (15 people or fewer) to allow for conversation. A moderator/reporter for each group should be identified beforehand and have some briefing on the techniques of moderating and synthesizing group discussion.

Some general guidelines should be provided on what to look for and what to ask should the conversation falter.

4. *Avoiding "dust-on-the-shelf" syndrome.* The fate of most campuswide reports is to land somewhere near the latest self-study on some dusty shelf of old dissertations. This conversation, however, is about the lifeblood of the institution—fulfilling its educational mission—and should have some uses determined beforehand. For example, it can be submitted jointly to the president, to the faculty governing group, and to the student government association for presentation to the entire community. The completed report can go to the community at one time. The report should have an understood purpose.

Institutions realize also that with existing structures, the educational goal of responsible citizenship cannot be met campuswide. The integration of an institutionwide civic education component will require that institutions (not just one department or office) consider what such a component means educationally. It touches on requirements for general education, faculty load, faculty development, requirements for graduation, assessment and evaluation, and a whole array of issues that define an institution. To begin the process, colleges and universities must commit themselves to the educational goal of developing civic responsibility in their students. This component goes beyond most existing public service and internship programs to include a wide array of courses, internships, volunteer activities, and class work that challenge students to (1) understand the public world around them, (2) observe firsthand how individual citizens, working alone or in tandem with others, can affect our shared lives, (3) reflect on the theory of the classroom in real-world situations, and (4) develop a commitment to community service. *It could mean a fundamental change in the way institutions approach education for all disciplines and in the way students learn.*

The campus conversation is the first step in the process of defining the role of higher education in preparation for citizenship. It will not be neat and tidy, but it will create a dialogue on campus that, it is hoped, thinks beyond major or discipline to the larger purposes of the academy.

Civic Skills

Thinking, talking, and acting like a citizen are different from thinking, talking, and acting like a private individual. When individuals move from the private to the public, the scope of roles and responsibilities changes. Take the environment, for example. If only one person littered, one could easily say that, in the scope of life, the harm is minimal. The real public problem comes when an individual realizes that his actions affect others and that individual actions may violate the collective good of all citizens. The process of taking others into account moves us from the private to the public. We are then in the public realm, and we need to know how to act as such.

Second, people develop an attitude about talk and listening that is different from "talking to ourselves." I can know what "I" know without you; I cannot know what "we" know unless a conversation takes place (Mathews 1985). The impetus to know what "we" think is the foundation for developing judgment and ultimately the political will to act.

Public participation requires that citizens have the ability to talk, listen, think, *and* act together for common purposes. What citizens learn from talking with each other are *new* ways of relating and working with others. Public talk is a prerequisite for public judgment, which requires both thinking and imagining. "Judgment is the ability to bring principles to particulars without reducing the particulars to simple instances" (Minnich 1988, p. 33). Political judgment requires the ability to think together with others about the right public course of action. It is not a solo activity but requires that others be recognized and acknowledged in the process. "The journey from private opinion to political judgment does not follow a road from prejudice to true knowledge; it proceeds from solitude to sociability" (Barber 1988, p. 199). Public judgment is the capacity to think with others about collective lives and actions. It requires the ability to talk or imagine with others different viewpoints and perspectives.

Talking, thinking, judging, and imagining are called for when taking the courage to act. Courage has been called *the* political virtue, because other skills become worthless without it (Denneny 1979, p. 274). The will to act or the courage to act can of course be individual in the doing. But in the public life, the courage to act comes after a conversation with others about a common problem. Anne Moody, who risked her safety to integrate a lunch counter in Mississippi, was acting as an individual, which required individual courage, but her *will* to act came after a dialogue (imagined or real) about the injustices of segregation. Mahatma Ghandi and Martin Luther

King, Jr., both had enormous personal courage, but their strength to act came from the community of fellow citizens. The collective rescue of their Jewish citizens by the Danes during World War II is a prime example of a community in action. Who in the country and how did they literally have the political will to act on behalf of a relatively small group of its citizens, and why was it not present in other countries?

> *Obviously there is no simple answer. It does not even necessarily follow that the Danes are men of greater faith or deeper piety than other west Europeans. . . . It is not so much that the Danes were Christians, as they were* human. *How many others were even that? The Danes were able to do what they did because they were able to make decisions that were based on clear convictions about which they all agreed and which were in accord with the inner truth of man's own rational nature, as well as in accordance with the fundamental law of God in the Old Testament as well as in the Gospel: Thou shalt love thy neighbor as thyself. The Danes were able to resist the cruel stupidity of Nazi anti-Semitism because this fundamental truth was* important *to them. And because they were willing, in unanimous and concerted action, to stake their lives on this truth. In a word,* such action becomes possible where fundamental truths are taken seriously (Merton 1971, p. 167).

Civic skills are active, not passive. They require, even in thinking, that individuals interact and be in "conversation" with each other. Unfortunately, in the world of an overactive media, citizens are often in a one-way conversation with their newspapers, their television sets, or even with political candidates. The staged versions of political debates that have emerged in recent years are thinly masked soliloquies with almost no room for interaction. This kind of societal reinforcement makes it inherent that people, especially younger citizens, have a place to practice their skills. The logical realities of the mobile society make town or community meetings all the more important, but so often the "city hall" brand of town meeting is dominated by the special interest of the day. Where can citizens come together to talk about the overall health and well-being of the community, not a narrow interest? Civic skills must be practiced to last. Higher education has a special opportunity not only to teach but also to convene.

Implications for Higher Education
For faculty

Faculty have many opportunities to play a critical role in helping students prepare for citizenship. A clear argument exists for students to have some common background on the nature of citizenship and the supporting democratic theory. It might best be done in an interdisciplinary course or through a combination of theory, practice, and reflection in several courses. As important as the facts, however, students need context. The structure of the classroom environment and interactions between faculty and students give definite signals about the political environment in that setting and call forth different responses from students. Classes that allow differing opinions to be undermined by either the instructor or other students indicate the inequality of voices in that "community." Equal voice is necessary for participatory democracy. Faculty should help students define their own views of citizenship, no matter what the discipline. Allowing students to relate to real-life situations—in scientific issues or using metaphor or example in literature classes—engages students in the practice of politics. Finally, the actual structure of the class mirrors a vision of politics. Lectures given with no input or discussion from students can create an authoritarian, passive learning environment but also denies students the opportunity to reflect verbally or in some instances mentally on the ideas presented. Further, the inflexibility across disciplines for joint programming or team teaching shows a lack of creativity and sends a negative signal about the value of working together. In the preparation of students for citizenship, faculty members are the facilitators. They do not indoctrinate; rather, they unpack knowledge while creating the "space" contextually, structurally, and intellectually for students to acknowledge, reflect, and practice the common life.

For administrators

The responsibility for civic preparation is even more direct for administrators than for faculty. Administrators interact with students and others on campus civically every day, offering a model of community. For example, a campus that holds diversity as a value should display it through its hiring practices throughout the institution, top to bottom. The importance of diversity is expressed in a less dramatic way with the treatment of nontraditional students. Campuses that make no

allowances for working adults, disabled students, or international students may be sending a "not-wanted" message. The
administration's relationship with the faculty is always head-
line news for the entire community. Students are quick to discern when relations are strained and when cross-purposes
exist within the academy. Just as the classroom structure
reflects the political, so does the governing structure. Finally,
the attitude of administrators toward students is an important
indicator of the civic model on campus. The joking remark,
"This would be a great place if it weren't for the students,"
is perhaps not a joke at some colleges and universities. The
respect shown by those in advising, admissions, records, student affairs, financial aid, and housing sets a tone for the institution. Inflexible hours, inefficient organization, and negative
personal interactions tell students that what they think, need,
or do is not valued. Programming for extracurricular activities
and for residential life is an important opportunity to present
new ways for people to live, work, and learn together if they
are designed as a means to learning. One should guard against
too many activities, however:

> Many of the well-intentioned administrative divisions super-
> vising nonacademic campus life now provide too many
> student services. [They] are often redundant and encour-
> age a passive attitude to campus involvement (Hrubala
> 1989, p. 53).

Higher education may be remiss in what it does and does not
do for students. If this hypothesis is correct, the overrespon-
siveness brought on by the sixties and seventies may have
limited students' ability to solve their own problems and their
participation in the real issues that influence their college
years and beyond.

Administrators, from the president up and down the organization chart, have the opportunity, however, to stimulate
and nourish a civic environment—not from services or
speeches, but from actions.

For students
Learning is ultimately students' responsibility. They have many
opportunities for developing civic skills—internships, special
outreach projects, and so on—that go unused. Students often
buy into a system of student government and extracurricular

activities that reflects old line political brokering and exclusivity. The way student politics is handled says much about the campus vision of the political or shared life. The campus is a place where students can participate in a shared life in a myriad of ways. The prominent vision of "politics" will determine how people perceive that things should be done and how they could be done. And interactions with fellow students—the social cliques, exclusive clubs, and shocking instances of clear racism—are reasons for helping students understand the importance of diversity in society, the need to respect differing opinions, and the essence of finding common ground with all people.

Higher education holds the master key for civic preparation of the next generation. Colleges and universities can open many doors for students, allowing them to refine and expand on their notions of politics and the common world. The problem is not about curriculum, not about governance, and not about student affairs. It is about the rest of students' lives and the community they will share with others.

Barber called on higher education to quit whining about what we are not and take action on what we are—a community dedicated to educating responsible, productive citizens. But as the literature has shown clearly, community is not about space or geography; it is about relationships.

> *The ideal university community would unify all aspects of the undergraduate education—namely, social, academic, and residential. One of the many benefits of a residential college where students spend their time socializing, studying, and being together is that constant contact allows [provides] a greater possibility of integrative mentality in its basic (communication, understanding, cooperation) and more highly developed (personal growth, academic progress, public service) forms* (Hrubala 1989, p. 34).

The civic life we should hope for is not what we are; it is what we could be. The stakes are very high. We know the prediction for the U.S. debt in the next few years is $2 trillion, which in anybody's book makes us a debtor nation. We know that one-quarter of the children in the country live in poverty and that a growing number of them do not live in a home at all. We know that racism and sexism are alive and well and, even more alarming, have gained footholds on college campuses from Michigan to New Hampshire to South Carolina. We know that health care in our nation is becoming prohibitively expensive for many Americans. We know that our environment is deteriorating quickly. We know that the reports from Eastern Europe and the Soviet Union reveal opportunities for democracy for the world that have not been seen in our lifetime. And we know that within this country we have the spirit, the expertise, and the wisdom to address and lessen these problems. We must mobilize the talents of young and old. The answers do not lie in traditional political solutions; they are too complex for that. Rather, the solutions will come from people who say it does not have to be this way, that together we can do better, that we *are* better. That is what citizenship is all about.

REFERENCES

The Educational Resources Information Center (ERIC) Clearinghouse on Higher Education abstracts and indexes the current literature on higher education for inclusion in ERIC's data base and announcement in ERIC's monthly bibliographic journal, *Resources in Education* (RIE). Most of these publications are available through the ERIC Document Reproduction Service (EDRS). For publications cited in this bibliography that are available from EDRS, ordering number and price code are included. Readers who wish to order a publication should write to the ERIC Document Reproduction Service, 3900 Wheeler Avenue, Alexandria, Virginia 22304. (Phone orders with VISA or MasterCard are taken at 800/227-ERIC or 703/823-0500.) When ordering, please specify the document (ED) number. Documents are available as noted in microfiche (MF) and paper copy (PC). If you have the price code ready when you call EDRS, an exact price can be quoted. The last page of the latest issue of *Resources in Education* also has the current cost, listed by code.

Adams, Frank. 1972. "Highlander Folk School: Getting Information, Going Back and Teaching It." *Harvard Educational Review* 42(4): 96–119.

American Association of Community and Junior Colleges (AACJC). 1989. "Civic Responsibility and the American Student." Washington, D.C.: Author.

Arendt, Hannah. 1958. *The Human Condition.* Chicago: Univ. of Chicago Press.

———. 1963. *Eichmann in Jerusalem: A Report on the Banality of Evil.* New York: Viking Press.

———. 1965. *On Revolution.* New York: Penguin Press.

———. 1968. *Between Past and Future: Eight Exercises in Political Thought.* New York: Penguin Press.

Argryis, C., and D. Schon. 1974. *Theory and Practice: Improving Professional Effectiveness.* San Francisco: Jossey-Bass.

Arnett, Ronald C. 1986. *Communication and Community: Implications of Martin Buber's Dialogue.* Carbondale, Ill.: Southern Univ. Press.

Astin, Alexander, et al. 1988. *The American Freshman: National Norms for 1988.* Los Angeles: Univ. of California at Los Angeles, Higher Education Research Institute. ED 303 133. 245 pp. MF–01; PC not available EDRS.

Atlas, James. 5 June 1988. "The Battle of the Books." *New York Times.*

Barber, Benjamin R. 1984. *Strong Democracy: Participatory Politics for a New Age.* Berkeley and Los Angeles: Univ. of California Press.

———. 1988. *The Conquest of Politics: Liberal Philosophy in Democratic Times.* Princeton, N.J.: Princeton Univ. Press.

———. Fall 1989. "The Civic Mission of the University." *Kettering Review:* 67–72.

Barker, Ernest. 1946. *The Politics of Aristotle.* London: Oxford Univ. Press.

Baum, Robert J., ed. 1979. *Ethics and Engineering Curricula.* New York: Hastings Center/Plenum Press.

Beiner, Ronald. 1983. *Political Judgment.* Chicago: Univ. of Chicago Press.

Bell, Mark A., and Edward Eddy. 1980. "Values Education: A Student's Perspective, An Administrator's Response." In *Rethinking College Responsibilities for Values.* New Directions for Higher Education No. 31. San Francisco: Jossey-Bass.

Bellah, Robert N., Richard Madsen, William M. Sullivan, Ann Swidler, and Steven M. Tipton. 1985. *Habits of the Heart: Individualism and Commitment in American Life.* Berkeley: Univ. of California Press.

Bennett, William J. 1980. "The Teacher, the Curriculum, and Values Education Development." In *Rethinking College Responsibilities for Values.* New Directions for Higher Education No. 31. San Francisco: Jossey-Bass.

Berger, Peter. 1977. *Facing Up to Modernity: Excursions in Society, Politics, and Religion.* New York: Basic Books.

Bernstein, R.J. 1986. *Religion and American Public Life.* Mahwah, N.J.: Paulist Press.

Bitzer, Lloyd F. 1978. "A Rhetoric and Public Knowledge." In *Rhetoric, Philosophy, and Literature: An Exploration,* edited by Don M. Burks. West Lafayette, Ind.: Purdue Univ. Press.

Bloom, Allan. 1983. "Our Listless Universities." *Change* 15(3): 29–35.

———. 1987. *The Closing of the American Mind.* New York: Simon & Schuster.

Bok, Derek. 1982. *Beyond the Ivory Tower.* Cambridge, Mass.: Harvard Univ. Press.

Boyer, Ernest. 1988. *College: The Undergraduate Experience in America.* New York: Harper & Row.

Boyer, Ernest L., and Fred M. Hechinger. 1981. *Higher Learning in the Nation's Service.* Washington, D.C.: Carnegie Foundation for the Advancement of Teaching. ED 212 206. 75 pp. MF–01; PC not available EDRS.

Boyer, Ernest L., and Arthur Levine. 1981. *A Quest for Common Learning.* Washington D.C.: Carnegie Foundation for the Advancement of Teaching.

Boyte, Harry C. 1989. *Commonwealth: A Return to Citizen Politics.* New York: Free Press.

Boyte, Harry, and Sara Evans. 1986. *Free Spaces: The Sources of Democratic Change in America.* New York: Harper & Row.

Brookfield, Stephen D. 1987. *Developing Critical Thinkers: Challenging Adults to Explore Alternative Ways of Thinking and Acting.* San Francisco: Jossey-Bass.

Brown, David. Spring 1986. "Civic Virtue in America." *Kettering Review:* 6–12.

Brown, Richard. 1986. *Revolutionary Politics in Massachusetts.* New York: W.W. Norton & Co.

Brubaker, John S. 1977. *On the Philosophy of Higher Education.* San Francisco: Jossey-Bass.

Brubaker, John S., and Willis Rudy. 1976. *Higher Education in Transition.* New York: Harper & Row.

Butts, Freeman. Winter 1982. "The Revival of Civic Learning Requires a Prescribed Curriculum." *Liberal Education* 68: 377–402.

Cadwallader, Mervyn L. 1983. "Education for Public Virtue." *Journal of Higher Education* 34(6): 41–44.

Callahan, Daniel, and Sissela Bok, eds. 1979. *The Teaching of Ethics in Higher Education.* New York: Hastings Center/Plenum Press.

Campus Compact. 1988. *Service Learning: An Annotated Bibliography.* Raleigh, N.C.: National Society for Internships and Experiential Education.

Canovan, Margaret. 1983. "Arendt, Rousseau, and Human Plurality in Politics." *Journal of Politics* 45(2): 286–301.

Carnegie Commission on Higher Education. 1973. *Purposes and Performances of Higher Education in the United States.* New York: McGraw-Hill.

Chiarelott, Leigh. 1979. "Dewey's Theory of Experience: An Application to Citizenship Education." *Social Studies* 70(2): 81–85.

Cleveland, Harlan. June 1981. "What's Higher about Higher Education." *Vital Speeches of the Day* 47: 509–12.

Coles, Robert. 1986. *The Political Life of Children.* Boston: Atlantic Monthly Press.

———. 1989a. *The Call of Stories.* Boston: Houghton Mifflin.

———. 1989b. "Learning by Doing through Public Service." *Change* 21(5): 18–26.

Coles, R., and T. Davey. 25 September 1976. "Young Activists of the 70s." *New Republic:* 14–16.

Cortes, Carlos. 1983. "The Mass Media: Civic Education's Public Curriculum." *Journal of Higher Education* 34(6): 25–29.

Couto, R.A. 1982. *Streams of Idealism and Health Care Innovation: An Assessment of Service Learning and Community Mobilization.* New York: Teachers College Press.

Cronin, Thomas E. 1989. *Direct Democracy.* Cambridge, Mass.: Harvard Univ. Press.

Curti, M. 1965. *The Social Ideas of American Educators.* Paterson, N.J.: Littlefield, Adams & Co.

Daley, J.S., and J.S. Pernaul. 1984. "Participation in and Benefits from Experiential Education." *Educational Record* 65(3): 18–23.

Denneny, Michael. 1979. "The Privilege of Ourselves: Hannah Arendt on Judgment." In *Hannah Arendt: The Recovery of the Public World,* edited by Melvin A. Hill. New York: St. Martin's Press.

DePree, Max. 1989. *Leadership Is an Art.* New York: Doubleday.

Dewey, John. 1909. *Moral Principles in Education.* Boston: Houghton Mifflin.

———. 1954. *The Public and Its Problems.* Athens, Ohio: Swallow Press.

Dickson, A. 1982. "A Service-Learning Retrospective." *Synergist* 2(1): 40–43.

Droskos, Charles C. 1988. *A Call to Civic Service.* New York: Free Press.

Ehman, L. 1980. "The American School in the Political Socialization Process." *Review of Educational Research* 50: 99–119.

Elliott, J. 1980. "Implications for Classroom Research for Professional Development." In *World Yearbook of Education.* London: Kogan Page.

Fleishman, Joel L., and Bruce L. Payne, eds. 1979. *Ethical Dilemmas and the Education of Policy Makers.* New York: Hastings Center/Plenum Press.

Flexner, Alexander. 1930. *Universities: English, German, and American.* New York: Oxford Univ. Press.

Follett, Mary Parker. 1920. *The New State: Group Organization, the Solution of Popular Government.* New York: Longmans, Green & Co.

Forum for Liberal Education. 1985. Special issue: "Promoting Civic Literacy" 7(4).

Fullinwider, R.K. Fall 1988. "Taking Ethics Seriously." *Civic Arts Review* 3.

Gagnon, Paul. 1988. "Why Study History?" *Atlantic* 262(5): 43–66.

Gardner, John. 1987. "The Moral Aspect of Leadership." Leadership Papers No. 5. Washington, D.C.: Independent Sector.

———. 1990. *On Leadership.* New York: Free Press.

Gelford, D.E., and J.P. Firman. 1981. "Developing and Implementing Service-Learning in Aging." *Educational Gerontology* 7: 2–3.

Giroux, Henry A. 1980. "Critical Theory and Rationality in Citizenship Education." *Curriculum Inquiry* 10(4): 329–66.

Glaser, Edward. 1985. "Critical Thinking: Education for Citizenship in a Democracy." *National Forum* 65(1): 24–27.

Goldberger, Leo, ed. 1987. *The Rescue of the Danish Jews.* New York: New York Univ. Press.

Goodlad, Sinclair. 1975. *Education and Social Action: Community Service and the Curriculum in Higher Education.* New York: Barnes & Noble.

Gordon, S.C. 1976. "Campus and Workplace as Arenas." In *Experiential Learning,* edited by Morris T. Keeton. San Francisco: Jossey-

Bass.

Greenleaf, Robert K. 1977. *Servant Leadership.* Mahwah, N.J.: Paulist Press.

Greenstein, Fred I. 1965. *Children and Politics.* New Haven, Conn.: Yale Univ. Press.

Gross, E., and P.V. Gambsch. 1974. *Changes in University Organization, 1964–1971.* New York: McGraw-Hill.

Habermas, Jurgen. 1985. *Critical Theory and Public Life,* edited by John Forester. Cambridge, Mass.: MIT Press.

Harding, G. 1974. "Nova: A Community Service/Education Experiment at the University of Nebraska." Lincoln: Univ. of Nebraska.

Heifetz, Ronald A., and Riley Sinder. 1988. *The Power of Public Ideas,* edited by Robert Reich. New York: Ballinger.

Hickman, F.M. 1982. "Education for Citizenship: Issues of Science and Society." *American Biology Teacher* 44(6): 358–65.

Hirsch, Eric David. 1987. *Cultural Literacy: What Every American Needs to Know.* Boston: Houghton Mifflin.

Hofer, B.R., R.F. Sexton, and E. Yarnella. 1976. "Exploring the Psycho-Political Development of Liberal Arts Interns." In *Initiating Experiential Learning Programs: Four Case Studies.* Princeton, N.J.: Educational Testing Service.

Howe, Irving. Fall 1988. "What Should We Be Teaching?" *Dissent* 35: 477–79.

Hrubala, Steven D. 1989. "The Student's Role in Educating for Citizenship." In *Public Leadership Education,* edited by Suzanne W. Morse. Dayton, Ohio: Kettering Foundation.

Hutchings, Pat, and Alan Wutzdorff. 1988. "Experiential Learning across the Curriculum: Assumptions and Principles." In *Knowing and Doing: Learning through Experience.* San Francisco: Jossey-Bass.

Hutchins, Robert M. 1974. *Higher Learning in America.* New Haven, Conn.: Yale Univ. Press.

Ignatieff, Michael. 1984. *The Needs of Strangers.* New York: Viking Penguin.

Jaeger, Werner. 1939. Paideia: *The Ideals of Greek Culture.* Vol. 1. New York: Oxford Univ. Press.

Janowitz, Morris. 1983. *The Reconstruction of Patriotism.* Chicago: Univ. of Chicago Press.

Jefferson, Thomas. 1903. *The Works of Thomas Jefferson,* edited by Paul Leichester Ford. 12 vols. New York: Knickerbocker Press.

Kant, Immanuel. 1951. *Critique of Judgment,* translated by J.H. Bernard. New York: Hafner Publishing.

Kateb, George. 1983. *Hannah Arendt: Politics, Conscience, Evil.* Totawa, N.J.: Rowman & Allenhead.

Kearney, Richard. 1988. *The Wake of Imagination: Toward a Post-*

modern Culture. Minneapolis: Univ. of Minnesota Press.

Kelly, George Armstrong. 1979. "Who Needs a Theory of Citizenship?" *Daedalus* 108(4): 21–36.

Kennedy, Donald. 1986. "'Can We Help?' Public Service and the Young." Paper presented at an annual meeting of the American Association for Higher Education, March, Washington, D.C. ED 270 001. 10 pp. MF–01; PC–01.

———. 1988. Flyer for the Stanford Service-Learning Institute. Stanford Univ.

Ketcham, Ralph. 1987. *Individualism and Public Life.* New York: Basil Blackwell, Inc.

Koch, Adrienne. 1964. *The Philosophy of Thomas Jefferson.* Chicago: Quadrangle Books.

Kolb, David. 1984. *Experiential Learning: Experience as the Source of Learning and Development.* Englewood Cliffs, N.J.: Prentice-Hall.

Landy, M., and W.C. McWilliams. 1985. "Civil Education in an Uncivil Culture." *Transaction* 22(3): 52–55.

Lasch, Christopher. 1978. *The Culture of Narcissism.* New York: W.W. Norton & Co.

Lazerson, Michael, Judith Block McLaughlin, and Bruce McPherson. 1984. "Learning and Citizenship: Aspirations for American Education." *Daedalus* 113(4): 59–74.

Levine, Arthur. 1980. *When Dreams and Heroes Died: A Portrait of Today's College Student.* San Francisco: Jossey-Bass.

Liberal Education. 1982. Special issue: "The Civic Purposes of Liberal Learning" 68(4).

Lipscomb, Andrew A., ed. 1903. *The Writings of Thomas Jefferson.* Washington, D.C.: Thomas Jefferson Memorial Association.

McBee, Mary Louise. 1980. "The Values Development Dilemma." In *Rethinking College Responsibilities for Values.* New Directions for Higher Education No. 31. San Francisco: Jossey-Bass.

McGrath, Earl. 1975. *Values, Liberal Education, and National Destiny.* Indianapolis, Ind.: Lilly Endowment.

McKenzie, Robert. Summer/Fall 1987. "Center Focus." *Antaeus Report:* 11–19.

Mansbridge, Jane J. 1980. *Beyond Adversary Democracy.* New York: Basic Books.

Mansfield, Harvey C., Jr. Spring 1984. "The Teaching of Citizenship." *PS* 17: 211–15.

Manz, Charles C., and Henry P. Sims, Jr. 1989. *Super Leadership.* Englewood Cliffs, N.J.: Prentice-Hall.

Mathews, David. Winter 1982. "The Liberal Arts and the Civic Arts." *Liberal Education* 68: 270–76.

———. November/December 1985. "Civic Intelligence." *Social Edu-*

cation 49: 678–81.

———. 1988. "Teaching Politics as Public Work: An Alternative Theory of Civic Education." Paper presented at an annual meeting of Citizenship for the 21st Century, October, Washington, D.C. ED 306 187. 10 pp. MF–01; PC–01.

———. 1989. "Teaching Politics as Public Work: An Alternative Theory of Civic Education." In *Public Leadership Education,* edited by Suzanne W. Morse. Dayton, Ohio: Kettering Foundation.

Matthews, Richard K. 1984. *The Radical Politics of Thomas Jefferson: A Revisionist View.* Lawrence: Univ. of Kansas Press.

Mayer, J.P., ed. 1969. *Democracy in America.* Garden City, N.Y.: Doubleday.

Merton, T. 1971. *The Nonviolent Alternative.* New York: Farrar Straus Giroux.

Miller, A. 1984. *For Your Own Good: Hidden Cruelty in Child-Rearing and the Roots of Violence.* New York: Farrar Straus Giroux.

Miller, Gary. 1988. *The Meaning of General Education: The Emergence of a Curricular Paradigm.* New York: Teachers College Press.

Mills, C. Wright. 1959. *The Sociological Imagination.* New York: Oxford Univ. Press.

Minnich, Elizabeth Kamarck. 1982. "Liberal Arts and the Civic Arts: Education for 'The Free Man?'" *Liberal Education* 68(4): 311–23.

———. Summer 1988. "Some Reflections on Civic Education and the Curriculum." *Kettering Review.*

Morrill, Richard L. 1980. *Teaching Values in College.* San Francisco: Jossey-Bass.

———. 1982. "Educating for Democratic Values." *Liberal Education* 68(4): 365–76.

Morse, Suzanne. 1988. "Developing a Capacity for Civic Judgment." In *Service Learning: A Resource for Community and Public Service.* Raleigh, N.C.: National Society for Internships and Experiential Education.

———. 1989a. "The Role of Colleges and Universities in Developing a New Brand of Public Leader." *National Civic Review* 78(6): 439–54.

———, ed. 1989b. *Public Leadership Education: Preparing College Students for Their Civic Roles.* Dayton, Ohio: Kettering Foundation.

Moskos, Charles C. 1988. *A Call to Civic Service: National Service for Country and Community.* New York: Free Press.

Muir, W.K. Winter 1983. *The TA at UCLA Newsletter* 10. Los Angeles: Univ. of California at Los Angeles.

Mumford, Lewis. 1961. *The City in History: Its Origins, Its Transformations, and Its Prospects.* New York: Harcourt Brace Jovanovich.

Murchland, Bernard. 1982. "Technology, Liberal Learning, and Civic Purpose." *Liberal Education* 68(4): 297–310.

———. 1983. "Citizenship in a Technological Society: Problems and Possibilities." *Journal of Higher Education* 34(6): 21–24.

———. 1988. "Educating for Citizenship." *Antaeus Report.*

National Society for Internships and Experiential Education (NSIEE). 1988. *Service Learning: An Annotated Bibliography.* Raleigh, N.C.: Author.

———. 1990. *Combining Service and Learning: A Resource Book for Community and Public Service.* Raleigh, N.C.: Author.

Neuhaus, Richard J. 1984. *The Naked Public Square.* Grand Rapids, Mich.: William B. Eerdmans Publishing Co.

Newman, Frank. 1985. *Higher Education and the American Resurgence.* Princeton, N.J.: Princeton Univ. Press.

Newman, Frank, Catharine Milton, and Susan Stroud. 1985. "Community Service and Higher Education: Obligations and Opportunities." *AAHE Bulletin* 37(10): 9–13. ED 261 635. 12 pp. MF–01; PC–01.

Nisbet, Robert. 1970. "The Total Community." In *Power in Societies,* edited by Marvin E. Olsen. New York: Macmillan.

Oliner, Samuel P., and Pearl M. Oliner. 1988. *The Altruistic Personality.* New York: Free Press.

Oliver, D.W., and J.P. Shaver. 1966. *Teaching Public Issues in the High School.* Boston: Houghton Mifflin.

Oliver, Leonard P. 1987. "Teaching Civic Values and Political Judgment in the Community College." In *Colleges of Choice,* edited by Judith Eaton. New York: Macmillan.

O'Neil, Edward H. 1987. "The Liberal Tradition of Civic Education." Working paper presented at the 16th Annual Conference of the National Society for Internships and Experiential Education, Vermont.

Palmer, Parker. 1981. *The Company of Strangers: Christians and the Renewal of America's Public Life.* New York: Crossroad Publishers.

———. 1987. "Community Conflict and Ways of Knowing: Ways to Deepen Our Educational Agenda." *Change* 19(5): 20–25.

Pateman, Carol. 1970. *Participation and Democratic Theory.* Cambridge, Eng.: Cambridge Univ. Press.

Paul, Richard. 1984. "Critical Thinking: Fundamental to Education for a Free Society." *Educational Leadership* 42(1): 4–14.

Peirce, Neal R. 1988. "A Public Trust: What Colleges and Universities Can—and Should—Do for Society." *Currents* 14(6): 9–14.

People for the American Way. 1988. *The Vanishing Voter and the Crisis in American Democracy.* Washington, D.C.: Author.

Pericles. 1811. "Funeral Oration." In *On the Peloponnesian War* [Thucydides], edited by Caroli Ludicovici Baveri. London: J. Parker,

Robert Abliss, T. Payne, and F.C. and J. Rivington. Passage translated by Peter Levine, 1987.

Phillips, Ellis. 1980. "Improving Decision Making in Business and the Professions." In *Rethinking College Responsibilities for Values.* New Directions for Higher Education No. 31. San Francisco: Jossey-Bass.

Pitkin, Hanna. 1981. "Justice: On Relating Public and Private." *Political Theory* 9(3): 327–52.

Pollock, Robert. 1960. "Process and Experience." In *John Dewey: His Thought and Influence,* edited by John Blewett. New York: Fordham Univ. Press.

Porter-Honnett, Ellen, and Susan Poulsen. October 1989. "Principles of Good Practice for Service-Learning." *Wingspread Journal.* Racine, Wis.: Johnson Foundation.

Reich, Richard, ed. 1988. *The Power of Public Ideas.* Cambridge, Mass.: Ballinger.

Reichley, A. James. 1985. *Religion in American Public Life.* Washington, D.C.: Brookings Institution.

Reische, Diana L. 1987. *Citizenship: Goal of Education.* Arlington, Va.: American Association of School Administrators.

Robbins, Richard, and Phillip DeVita. 1985. "Anthropology and the Teaching of Human Values." *Anthropology and Education Quarterly* 16: 251–56.

Rockfish Gap Commission. 1961. "Report of the Rockfish Gap Commission [1818] Appointed to Fix the Site of the University of Virginia." In *American Higher Education: A Documentary History,* edited by Richard Hofstader and Wilson Smith. Vol. 1. Chicago: Univ. of Chicago Press.

Roosevelt, Theodore. 1956. *The Free Citizen: A Summons to Service of the Democratic Ideal,* edited by Hermann Hagedorn. New York: Macmillan.

Rousseau, Jean-Jacques. 1964. *The First and Second Discourses,* edited by Roger Masters and translated by Roger D. Masters and Judith R. Masters. New York: St. Martin's Press.

———. 1974. *The Social Contract: Or Principles of Political Right,* edited and translated by Charles M. Sherover. New York: New American Library.

Rutgers University. 1989. "Final Report to the Committee on Education for Civic Leadership on a Program of Citizen Education and Community Service for Rutgers University, 1989." New Brunswick, N.J.: Author.

Sartori, Giovanni. 1987. *The Theory of Democracy Revisited.* Chatham: Chatham House.

Schlesinger, Arthur M., Jr. 1986. *The Cycles of American History.* Boston: Houghton Mifflin.

Schultz, Steven K. 1987. "Learning by Heart: The Role of Action in

Civic Education." Paper presented at the 16th Annual Conference of the National Society for Internships and Experiential Education, Vermont.

Schumpeter, Joseph. 1950. *Capitalism, Socialism, and Democracy.* 3d ed. New York: Harper & Row.

Sennett, Richard. 1977. *The Fall of Public Man.* New York: Alfred A. Knopf.

Simonson, R., and S. Walker. 1988. *Multicultural Literacy: Opening of the American Mind.* St. Paul, Minn.: Graywolf Press.

Sloan, Douglas. December 1977. "The Higher Learning and Social Vision." *Teachers College Record* 79: 163–69.

Smith, Jonathan. November/December 1987. "Playful Acts of Imagination." *Liberal Education* 74: 14–20.

Southern Regional Education Board. 1973. *Service-Learning in the South: Higher Education and Public Service, 1967–1972.* Atlanta: Author.

Spitzberg, Irving. 1986. "Campus Programs on Leadership." Washington, D.C.: Association of American Colleges, Council on Liberal Learning.

Stanley, Manfred. 1989. "The American University as a Civic Institution." *Civic Arts Review* 2(2): 4–9.

Stanton, Charles. 1986. "A View from the Portico: Lessons from the Greeks." Paper presented at an annual meeting of the Association for the Study of Higher Education, February, San Antonio, Texas. ED 268 889. 20 pp. MF–01; PC–01.

Sullivan, William M. 1982. *Reconstructing Public Philosophy.* Berkeley: Univ. of California Press.

Tocqueville, Alexis de. 1956. *Democracy in America,* edited by Richard D. Heffner. New York: New American Library.

Toufexis, Anastasia. 16 March 1987. "Silver Bullets for the Needy." *Time.*

Tyson, Ruel. 1988. "Teaching Political Education." *Civic Arts Review* 1(1): 10–12.

Walzer, Michael. 1971. *Obligations: Essays on Disobedience, War, and Citizenship.* New York: Simon & Schuster.

———. 1980. *Radical Principles: Reflections of an Unreconstructed Democrat.* New York: Basic Books.

Ward, Champion. 1989. "A Requiem for Hutchins College." *Change* 21(4): 25–33.

Warwick, Donald P., ed. 1979. *The Teaching of Ethics in the Social Sciences.* New York: Hastings Center/Plenum Press.

Wegener, Charles. 1978. *Liberal Education and the Modern University.* Chicago: Univ. of Chicago Press.

Weissberg, Robert. 1974. *Political Learning, Political Choice, and Democratic Citizenship.* Englewood Cliffs, N.J.: Prentice-Hall.

Wolff, Robert Paul. 1970. *The Ideal of the University.* Boston: Beacon Press.

Yankelovich, Daniel. 1985. "How the Public Learns the Public's Business." *Kettering Review:* 8–18.

Young-Bruehl, Elizabeth. 1982. "Reflections on Hannah Arendt's *The Life of the Mind.*" *Political Theory* 10(2).

————. 1989. *Mind and the Body Politic.* New York: Rutledge, Chapman & Hall.

Zuckerman, Michael. 1970. *Peaceable Kingdom: New England Towns in the Eighteenth Century.* New York: Alfred A. Knopf.

INDEX

A

Academic and public life, 99
Adler, Mortimer, 34
African-Americans, 32, 60
Alienation, 1
Alverno College, 40
American citizenship
 history of, 10
Ancient Greece, 8, 10, 12, 71, 82
Antioch College, 86
Apartheid, 77
Apprenticeships, 84
Arendt, Hannah, 3, 11, 71, 73, 84, 83
Aristotle, 5, 71
Athenians, 8, 101
Athens, 9

B

Babson College, 55
Baruch College, 55
Bellow, Saul, 52
Bennett, William, 88
Berea College, 86
Bill of Rights, 5
Brown University, 39–40
Brown v. Board of Education, 32
Burke, Edmund, 10-11

C

Campus Compact Project for Public and Community Service, 39
Campus Outreach Opportunity League (COOL), 39
Carnegie Commission on Higher Education. 33, 38
Center for Health Services, 84
Center for the Study of Philanthropy, 55
Centers for Public Service, 40
Christianity, 10
"Citizen apprentice", 84
Citizen participation, 8
Citizen responsibilities, 1, 4
Citizens
 withdrawal, 21
Citizenship, 5
 Jeffersonian notion of, 17
 modern, 6
 new definitions of, 14
 preparing students for, 34
 skills, 59

City University of New York, 55
Civic associations, 16
Civic consciousness, 6
Civic conversation, 101–102
Civic education
    experiential, 95
    reflective. 95
    theoretical, 95
Civic leadership education, 27, 52
Civil Rights Act of 1965, 77
Civilian Conservation Corps, 44
Civic skills, 67, 103
Classical education, 34–38
Coles, Robert, 59
College of William and Mary, 28
"Common good", 7
Commonwealth, 17
Community colleges, 32
Community service, 38
Constitution (U.S.), 5, 90
Cooperative learning, 86
Courage, 75, 104
Cultural traditions, 34
Curriculum, 49, 50, 68, 99

D

"Debtbusters", 89
Declaration of Independence, 36, 90
Democracy
    electoral competitive, 62
    participatory, 62
    representative, 62
"Democracy of the club", 8
Democratic statecraft, 78
Denmark, 75
Department of Defense, 19
Dewey, John, 1, 18, 20, 39, 54, 85
Direct democracy, 8, 11, 24

E

Economics, 22
Education
    service based, 38–43
Education Commission of the States, 29
Educational summit, 41
Eichmann. Adolph, 73
Electoral system, 64
Environment, 109

Ethics, 55–56
Experiential education, 85–86

F

"Fellow feeling", 3
Flexner, Alexander, 30
Franklin, Benjamin, 28
Free spaces, 15

G

Gardner, John, 43, 45
Georgetown University, 39
Great Books, 35, 37, 88

H

Harper, William Raney, 31
Harvard University, 47
Health care, 109
Henry Luce Foundation, 45
Higher Education
      and citizenship, 99–100
      civic preparation, 108
      implications for administrators, 106
      implications for faculty, 106
      implications for students, 107
      role in civic education, 27
Highlander Folk School, 94
Historicism, 36
Holocaust, 73
Horton, Miles, 94
Humphrey Institute, 45
Hutchins, Robert, 34

I

Imagination, 74
Indiana University, 55
Internships, 85-87

J

Jefferson, Thomas, 10–12, 54, 81, 90
Jeffersonian democracy, 2
Johnson Foundation, 43
Judeo-Christian tradition, 13

K

Kantian philosophy, 71, 73, 82
Kings College, 28

Koinonia, 8

L

Leadership studies, 43–49
Liberal arts, 49

M

Mandela, Nelson, 77
Mather, Cotton, 27
Military-industrial complex, 21
Minorities, 4
Morrill Act, 31

N

National debt, 108
National Service Bill, 44
National Society for Internships and Experiential Education, 39, 101
Neoconservatives, 15–16
Newman, Cardinal, 34

P

Participatory democracy, 66
Peace Corps, 44
Pendle Hill, 54
Pericles, 3
Philanthropic studies, 55
Plato, 9, 82
"Platoons of democracy", 89
Polis, 4, 8, 9, 13, 19
Political judgment, 70–71
Political life, 22–23, 61
Political talk, 67–69
Politics
        classical notion, 3
        practice, 11, 82–83
Precollegiate education, 29
Primary education, 29
Private responsibilities, 18
Proposition 13, 13
Public
        definition of, 20
Public duties, 18
Public judgment, 71
Public life
        and academia, 99
        definition, 102
        educating for, 81
Public schools, 29

Public space, 3, 8

R

Racism, 108
Reformation, 10
Religious institutions
        role of, 13
Representative democracy, 65
Rockfish Gap Commission, 28
Roosevelt center, 89
Roosevelt, Theodore, 3
Rousseau, Jean-Jacques, 6, 12
Rutgers University, 40

S

Santayana, George, 88
Secondary education, 29
Service-based education, 42
Sexism, 108
Southern Christian Leadership Conference, 77
Southern Regional Education Board, 38
Special interests, 7, 18
Stanford University, 88
State Student Incentive Grant Programs, 44

T

Thinking, 69–70
Tocqueville, Alexis de, 2, 8, 14, 28
Town meetings, 10–12
Traditions, 21
Two-year colleges (see Community colleges)
Tufts University, 55

U

University as a community, 92
University of Chicago, 31
University of Richmond, 45
University of Southern California, 55
University of Virginia, 28, 41

V

Vanderbilt University, 84
VISTA, 44
Voluntary associations, 15
Voting statistics, 1
Voting decline, 78

W

ASHE-ERIC HIGHER EDUCATION REPORTS

Since 1983, the Association for the Study of Higher Education (ASHE) and the Educational Resources Information Center (ERIC) Clearinghouse on Higher Education, a sponsored project of the School of Education and Human Development at The George Washington University, have cosponsored the *ASHE-ERIC Higher Education Report* series. The 1989 series is the eighteenth overall and the first to be published by the School of Education and Human Development at the George Washington University.

Each monograph is the definitive analysis of a tough higher education problem, based on thorough research of pertinent literature and insitutional experiences. Topics are identified by a national survey. Noted practitioners and scholars are then commissioned to write the reports, with experts providing critical reviews of each manuscript before publication.

Eight monographs (10 before 1985) in the ASHE-ERIC Higher Education Report series are published each year and are available on individual and subscription basis. Subscription to eight issues is $80.00 annually; $60 to members of AAHE, AIR, or AERA; and $50 to ASHE members. All foreign subscribers must include an additional $10 per series year for postage.

Prices for single copies, including book rate postage, are $15.00 regular and $11.25 for members of AERA, AIR, AAHE, and ASHE ($10.00 regular and $7.50 for members for 1985 to 1987 reports, $7.50 regular and $6.00 for members for 1983 and 1984 reports, $6.50 regular and $5.00 for members for reports published before 1982). All foreign orders must include $1.00 per book for foreign postage. Fast United Parcel Service or first class postage is available for $1.00 per book in the U.S. and $2.50 per book outside the U.S. (orders above $50.00 may substitute 5% of the total invoice amount for domestic postage). Make checks payable to ASHE-ERIC. For VISA and MasterCard payments, include card number, expiration date, and signature. Orders under $25 must be prepaid. Bulk discounts are available on orders of 15 or more reports (not applicable to subscription orders). Order from the Publications Department, ASHE-ERIC Higher Education Reports, The George Washington University, One Dupont Circle, Suite 630, Washington, DC 20036-1183, or phone us at (202) 296-2597. Write for a complete catalog of all available reports.

1989 ASHE-ERIC Higher Education Reports

1. Making Sense of Administrative Leadership: The 'L' Word in Higher Education
   Estela M. Bensimon, Anna Neumann, and Robert Birnbaum

2. Affirmative Rhetoric, Negative Action: African-American and Hispanic Faculty at Predominantly White Universities
   Valora Washington and William Harvey

3. Postsecondary Developmental Programs: A Traditional Agenda with New Imperatives
   Louise M. Tomlinson

4. The Old College Try: Balancing Athletics and Academics in Higher Education
   John R. Thelin and Lawrence L. Wiseman

5. The Challenge of Diversity: Involvement or Alienation in the Academy?
   Daryl G. Smith

6. Student Goals for College and Courses: A Missing Link in Assessing and Improving Academic Achievement
   Joan S. Stark, Kathleen M. Shaw, and Malcolm A. Lowther

7. The Student-as-Commuter: Developing a Comprehensive Institutional Response
   Barbara Jacoby

1988 ASHE-ERIC Higher Education Reports

1. The Invisible Tapestry: Culture in American Colleges and Universities
   George D. Kuh and Elizabeth J. Whitt

2. Critical Thinking: Theory, Research, Practice, and Possibilities
   Joanne Gainen Kurfiss

3. Developing Academic Programs: The Climate for Innovation
   Daniel T. Seymour

4. Peer Teaching: To Teach is To Learn Twice
   Neal A. Whitman

5. Higher Education and State Governments: Renewed Partnership, Cooperation, or Competition?
   Edward R. Hines

6. Entrepreneurship and Higher Education: Lessons for Colleges, Universities, and Industry
   James S. Fairweather

7. Planning for Microcomputers in Higher Education: Strategies for the Next Generation
   Reynolds Ferrante, John Hayman, Mary Susan Carlson, and Harry Phillips

8. The Challenge for Research in Higher Education: Harmonizing Excellence and Utility
   Alan W. Lindsay and Ruth T. Neumann

1987 ASHE-ERIC Higher Education Reports

1. Incentive Early Retirement Programs for Faculty: Innovative Responses to a Changing Environment
   Jay L. Chronister and Thomas R. Kepple, Jr.

2. Working Effectively with Trustees: Building Cooperative Campus Leadership
   Barbara E. Taylor

3. Formal Recognition of Employer-Sponsored Instruction: Conflict and Collegiality in Postsecondary Education
   Nancy S. Nash and Elizabeth M. Hawthorne

4. Learning Styles: Implications for Improving Educational Practices
   Charles S. Claxton and Patricia H. Murrell

5. Higher Education Leadership: Enhancing Skills through Professional Development Programs
   Sharon A. McDade

6. Higher Education and the Public Trust: Improving Stature in Colleges and Universities
   Richard L. Alfred and Julie Weissman

7. College Student Outcomes Assessment: A Talent Development Perspective
   Maryann Jacobi, Alexander Astin, and Frank Ayala, Jr.

8. Opportunity from Strength: Strategic Planning Clarified with Case Examples
   Robert G. Cope

1986 ASHE-ERIC Higher Education Reports

1. Post-tenure Faculty Evaluation: Threat or Opportunity?
   Christine M. Licata

2. Blue Ribbon Commissions and Higher Education: Changing Academe from the Outside
   Janet R. Johnson and Laurence R. Marcus

3. Responsive Professional Education: Balancing Outcomes and Opportunities
   Joan S. Stark, Malcolm A. Lowther, and Bonnie M.K. Hagerty

4. Increasing Students' Learning: A Faculty Guide to Reducing Stress among Students
   Neal A. Whitman, David C. Spendlove, and Claire H. Clark

5. Student Financial Aid and Women: Equity Dilemma?
   Mary Moran

6. The Master's Degree: Tradition, Diversity, Innovation   -
   Judith S. Glazer

7. The College, the Constitution, and the Consumer Student: Implications for Policy and Practice
   Robert M. Hendrickson and Annette Gibbs

8. Selecting College and University Personnel: The Quest and the Question
   Richard A. Kaplowitz

1985 ASHE-ERIC Higher Education Reports

1. Flexibility in Academic Staffing: Effective Policies and Practices
   Kenneth P. Mortimer, Marque Bagshaw, and Andrew T. Masland

2. Associations in Action: The Washington, D.C. Higher Education Community
   Harland G. Bloland

3. And on the Seventh Day: Faculty Consulting and Supplemental Income
   Carol M. Boyer and Darrell R. Lewis

4. Faculty Research Performance: Lessons from the Sciences and Social Sciences
   John W. Creswell

5. Academic Program Review: Institutional Approaches, Expectations, and Controversies
   Clifton F. Conrad and Richard F. Wilson

6. Students in Urban Settings: Achieving the Baccalaureate Degree
   Richard C. Richardson, Jr. and Louis W. Bender

7. Serving More Than Students: A Critical Need for College Student Personnel Services
   Peter H. Garland

8. Faculty Participation in Decision Making: Necessity or Luxury?
   Carol E. Floyd

1984 ASHE-ERIC Higher Education Reports

1. Adult Learning: State Policies and Institutional Practices
   K. Patricia Cross and Anne-Marie McCartan

2. Student Stress: Effects and Solutions
   Neal A. Whitman, David C. Spendlove, and Claire H. Clark

3. Part-time Faulty: Higher Education at a Crossroads
   Judith M. Gappa

4. Sex Discrimination Law in Higher Education: The Lessons of the Past Decade
   J. Ralph Lindgren, Patti T. Ota, Perry A. Zirkel, and Nan Van Gieson

5. Faculty Freedoms and Institutional Accountability: Interactions and Conflicts
   Steven G. Olswang and Barbara A. Lee

6. The High Technology Connection: Academic/Industrial Cooperation for Economic Growth
   Lynn G. Johnson

7. Employee Educational Programs: Implications for Industry and Higher Education
   Suzanne W. Morse

8. Academic Libraries: The Changing Knowledge Centers of Colleges and Universities
   Barbara B. Moran

9. Futures Research and the Strategic Planning Process: Implications for Higher Education
   James L. Morrison, William L. Renfro, and Wayne I. Boucher

10. Faculty Workload: Research, Theory, and Interpretation
    Harold E. Yuker

1983 ASHE-ERIC Higher Education Reports

1. The Path to Excellence: Quality Assurance in Higher Education
   Laurence R. Marcus, Anita O. Leone, and Edward D. Goldberg

2. Faculty Recruitment, Retention, and Fair Employment: Obligations and Opportunities
   John S. Waggaman

3. Meeting the Challenges: Developing Faculty Careers*
   Michael C.T. Brooks and Katherine L. German

4. Raising Academic Standards: A Guide to Learning Improvement
   Ruth Talbott Keimig

5. Serving Learners at a Distance: A Guide to Program Practices
   Charles E. Feasley

6. Competence, Admissions, and Articulation: Returning to the Basics in Higher Education
   Jean L. Preer

7. Public Service in Higher Education: Practices and Priorities
   Patricia H. Crosson

8. Academic Employment and Retrenchment: Judicial Review and Administrative Action
   Robert M. Hendrickson and Barbara A. Lee

9. Burnout: The New Academic Disease*
   Winifred Albizu Melendez and Rafael M. de Guzmán

10. Academic Workplace: New Demands, Heightened Tensions
    Ann E. Austin and Zelda F. Gamson

*Out-of-print. Available through EDRS. Call 1-800-227-ERIC.